T0303371

PRAISE FOR *WAVE WOMAN*

"There are some people who venture into uncharted territory. They are referred to as pioneers, and that they are. In the world of surfing, one such pioneer was Betty. She was prominent, accomplished, and a champion surfer when women were not supposed to surf. She also ventured into bigger waves when most others were content to watch. Every young woman enjoying surfing in contemporary times should remember and appreciate Betty Heldreich. She made it 'happen.'"

—Fred Hemmings, author, keynote speaker, and
former surfing champion

"Betty Heldreich Winstedt was a lover of the ocean and a true surfing pioneer whose experiences in California and Hawaii were exceptional for the mid-1950s. *Wave Woman* is daughter Vicky's heartfelt tribute to this capable, gifted woman who taught those around her to live in the moment. 'Wake up and be somebody,' Betty would challenge—advice that resonates soundly today."

—Jane Schmauss, historian and founding member of
the California Surf Museum

"*Wave Woman* is a heartfelt tale about an inspiring surf pioneer. Betty Heldreich approached her life as a grand adventure, and Wave Woman captures her trailblazing triumphs and struggles."

—David Davis, author of *Waterman: The Life and Times of
Duke Kahanamoku*

"When Vicky Durand's mother spurned 1950s America for the life of a surfer in Waikiki and then Makaha, she plunged her daughter Vicky into a world of wonder. . . . Pick up *Wave Woman* and you'll enter that dreamtime in such exquisite, evocative detail that it may cause painful surges of nostalgia for what's been lost. But what you'll gain by reading Vicky's wise study of a painful marriage and a woman's need to express herself in the ocean could also inform your own life and those you love."

—Don Wallace, senior editor of *Honolulu Magazine*

"Reading Vicky Durand's *Wave Woman* made me wish that I had met her mother, Betty, in person. But by the end of the book, I realized that I had met this extraordinary woman, because Betty's gentle personality and fierce spirit come alive in this story. A surfing pioneer, Betty rode the turbulent waves of her life with grace and style. *Wave Woman* is a moving tribute to an amazing woman."

—Stuart H. Coleman, award-winning author of *Eddie Would Go, Fierce Heart*, and *Hawaiian Hero*

WAVE WOMAN

WAVE WOMAN

THE LIFE AND STRUGGLES
OF A SURFING PIONEER

Betty Pembroke Heldreich Winstedt (1913–2011)

Vicky Heldreich Durand

SPARKPRESS

Copyright © 2020 by Vicky Helderich Durand

All rights reserved, including the right to reproduce this book or portions thereof in any form whatsoever.

Published by SparkPress, a BookSparks imprint,
A division of SparkPoint Studio, LLC
Phoenix, Arizona, USA, 85007
www.gosparkpress.com

Published 2020
Printed in Canada
ISBN: 978-1-68463-042-4 (pbk)
ISBN: 978-1-68463-043-1 (e-bk)

Library of Congress Control Number: 2019912670

Interior design by Tabitha Lahr

All company and/or product names may be trade names, logos, trademarks, and/or registered trademarks and are the property of their respective owners.

Names and identifying characteristics have been changed

For all the women who have surfed,
and who will surf, in Betty's wake

CONTENTS

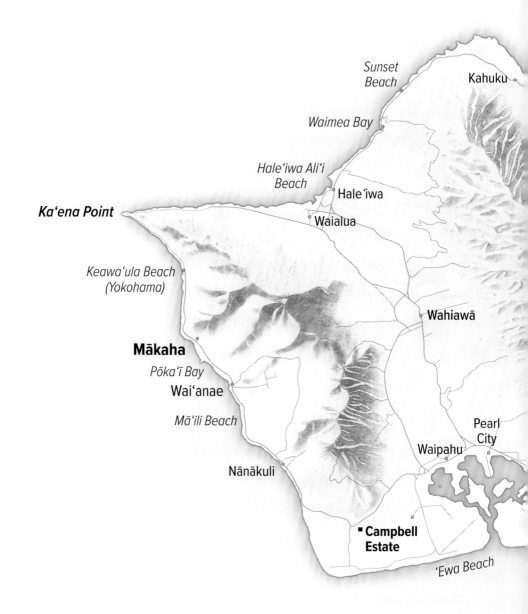

Sunset
Beach

Kahuku

Waimea Bay

Hale'iwa Ali'i
Beach

Hale'iwa

Ka'ena Point

Waialua

Keawa'ula Beach
(Yokohama)

Wahiawā

Mākaha

Pōka'ī Bay

Wai'anae

Mā'ili Beach

Pearl
City

Waipahu

Nānākuli

Campbell
Estate

'Ewa Beach

O'ahu, 1960

Kailua

ea

Honolulu

Willer's House

WAIKIKI

[Detail map on page 48]

Diamond Head

Ford's House

Koko Head

FOREWORD

To me, Betty Heldreich was Makaha in its positive aspects. In 1958, when I came to Hawaii to teach at Punahou, the historic private school in Honolulu, I got to know Betty's oldest daughter, Vicky, who had won the Makaha contest the year before and was a senior at Punahou. Through Vicky, I became good friends with Betty. The Heldreichs had a home adjacent to Makaha's surfing beach. Whenever I came to surf on the weekend, Betty let me park my old woody station wagon (with a mattress in the back) on their front lawn. I could look out at the surf break from my overnight perch. During those pleasant visits, Betty and I would talk about our times in Santa Monica, where I grew up and where Betty lived after graduating from USC.

Although Betty was there in the 1930s during the Depression and I was there later, we had a lot in common. We were both competitive swimmers and had mutual friends in the swimming world and on the beach. We shared a friendship with Pete Peterson, a lifeguard and probably the best all-around waterman of the twentieth century. Another old-timer who swam with Betty for the Los Angeles Athletic Club was Paul Wolf, the USC swim coach when I was competing at Stanford. My Stanford swim coach, Tom Haynie, had competed against Paul while at the University of Michigan in 1960 and came to Punahou, where he coached swimming for twenty years. Both Paul and Tom knew and admired Betty as a successful all-around water girl.

When Betty swam for the Los Angeles Athletic Club, she found herself among some of the best swimmers and water polo players in the world. During different decades, we both swam laps on our own and, coincidentally, at the Uplifters Club in Santa Monica Canyon—Betty in the 1930s, and I in the 1940s. Even though we were fifteen years apart, Santa Monica for both of us was a wonderful place to grow up. Fellow Santa Monicans like Buzzy Trent, Kit Horn, and Matt Kivlin started surfing in 1941 and mentored Corny, my twin brother, and me. Buzzy, along with George Downing and Wally Froiseth, became the best big Makaha Point surfers at the time, while Betty and her good friend Ethel Kukea were establishing themselves as early haole women to surf Makaha. Buzzy, George, and Wally admired Betty and Ethel and became their friends.

If Betty and I shared a bond because of Santa Monica, what really cemented our friendship was our love of the ocean and beaches at Makaha (where Betty lived and brought up her family) and Sunset Beach (where I have lived and brought up my family).

Betty remains always in my mind a one-of-a-kind person. She inspired men and women alike with her athleticism, her humility, and her fierce independence.

—Peter Cole, Sunset Beach, Hawaii

INTRODUCTION

THE BIG ARC OF BETTY'S LIFE

Laugh

Build for yourself a strong box,
Fashion each part with care;
When it's strong as your hand can make it,
Put all your troubles there;
Hide there all thought of your failures,
And each bitter cup of that you quaff;
Lock all your heartaches within it,
Then sit on the lid and laugh.
Tell no one else its contents,
Never its secrets share;
When you've dropped in your care and worry
Keep them forever there;
Hide them from sight so completely
That the world will never dream half;
Fasten the strong box securely
Then sit on the lid and laugh.

—Bertha Adams Backus, 1911

In August of 2015, I was looking for clues to the mystery of my mother's life. I knew the outlines: She came from pioneer stock in Utah, she fled a middle-class family life in Chino, she fell in love with surfing at age forty, she outlived two husbands and a few lovers. She was and is admired by surfers worldwide. She died at ninety-eight. But then I discovered a tattered cardboard box hidden on a dusty shelf in our Makaha Beach garage. The receptacle contained a forgotten trove: what my mother called her "autobiography"—written to cover her years from birth to age twenty-four—along with her collection of memorabilia, letters, and photos spanning the rest of her long life. Among the contents was a poem, "Laugh," by Bertha Adams Backus, which my mother had hand-copied on a small piece of paper and safeguarded for more than eighty years.

The poem captured my mother's philosophy; in fact, she lived her life in accordance with its tenets. Rather than exposing her fears, her failures, or her heartaches—to others and especially to her children—she kept them locked away. Additional letters and poems revealed details of her life we had never talked about.

Betty Pembroke Heldreich Winstedt was born in 1913 and died in 2011. Her secret writing projects recount a life that shows a spirit of adventure—indeed, a daring that continued into her last years. I wrestled the awkwardly heavy cardboard box off the garage shelf several years after she died. My mistake in not having asked my mother many more questions had just started to sink in.

To fill in the gaps, I embarked on a dual journey of discovery. The first part of my quest was to find more detailed information about my mother's unusual life and to learn more by writing about it. The second part was to learn how my mother's unconventional yet stoic example shaped others—and, of course, me.

At an early age, my mother developed a love of challenge that was unusual for a girl during the 1920s. She undertook projects—whether a pilot's license or a career in dentistry—that were the province of men. She possessed derring-do, and she dreamed big. She loved to learn how things worked and believed that it is never too late to expand one's horizons.

My mother worked ferociously and created relentlessly, but she was ready to play at the end of a day. She always had a project on the horizon, vocationally and avocationally: She was a dental hygienist, competitive swimmer, aviator, jeweler, pioneer surfer, house builder, potter, and haiku poet. She possessed an unwavering belief that she could start a dental lab, clean watches, take and develop photographs (in color, as well as black and white), and carve miniature objects out of wax. She never settled for less, and she taught me and others to do the same. "A little advice," she wrote in one of her haiku. "Wake up and be somebody. Don't be just a drudge."

"I grew up and lived in what I thought was one of the most beautiful places in existence: Salt Lake City," she wrote in her fourteen-page autobiography, which was folded and frayed by the time I discovered it in her garage. "I loved the softness and freshness of the air, the sweep of the valley right up to the Wasatch Range with the purple and pink colors at sunset. As a small girl, I thought it was such a joy to smell the blossoming trees that lined the streets."

At age five, Mother vacationed in Santa Monica with her paternal grandparents, Herbert and Sara Pembroke. When she laid eyes on the Pacific Ocean, she fell in love, infatuated with the sand between her toes, the shades of blue in the water, and the waves that crashed onshore. From that point forward, most of the choices in her life moved her inevitably closer to the waves.

I, too, had a similar transforming moment when, as an adolescent, I spent the summer with my aunt Jane and uncle Smithy on the island of Molokai. After that summer, I knew that I would never again be happy in landlocked Chino, California. I had to live near that ocean.

Two years later, in 1954, I was fourteen and my mother forty when we learned to surf at Waikiki, guided by the beach boy Charlie Amalu. We both took to the sport. Barely three years later, my mother was on the first Hawaiian surf team invited to Lima, Peru. In 1957, I won the Makaha International Surfing Contest. My mother and I were twenty-seven years apart, but more than genes brought us together: We were women thrilled by the challenge of the waves, the power of the ocean, and the search for adventure.

We both surfed Waikiki during what became known as the golden age of Hawaiian surfing. It was a romantic era, and we considered ourselves lucky to be part of it. My mother was one of the early haole (non-Hawaiian) women to surf the big waves at Makaha in modern times, earning herself the moniker of a surfing "pioneer."

I wrote down some of my mother's stories as she told them to me. Others I've pieced together from memory, news stories, and the accounts of her contemporaries. But, of course, the greatest resource has been the material from the box. Woven into my account are photos, letters, and memorabilia from her life as an artist. Also included are whimsical haiku she composed in her nineties to express an inner life that had always buoyed her but that she rarely shared. In the succinct, unrhymed verses (seventeen syllables with three lines, each divided into five, seven, and five syllables), she set down an observation of a vivid incident of daily life. The haiku is unassuming, a moment of truth waiting to be fully discovered.

My mother's poetry is the manifestation of her late-in-life reflections; she composed most of the haiku while facing the ocean at her Makaha Beach home. By then, she had lost nearly all her eyesight. Her poems are often humorous but also contain visions of the world she had known, yet could no longer see. In 2007, haiku, a brief life story, and pictures were assembled in a book, *Haiku of Life: A Surfer's Memories and Reflections*. A year later, the book was revised with new poems.

> Surfing is great fun
> Riding speed of the water
> Conquering one's fear
>
> —Betty, 2009

I am giving this material fresh form, seeing anew my mother's choice to approach obstacles with a positive attitude, inner strength, and courage. To begin, I offer her words from an afternoon in 1960, while we sat together at Makaha and she told me the story of nearly meeting her "Waterloo." (She called all her brushes with death her Waterloos.) As usual, she spoke calmly as she recalled the details.

It was the spring of 1959, a picture-perfect Hawaiian morning at Makaha Beach. Perfectly shaped, glassy waves rolled in from the point. The musty smell of saltwater-drenched kukui nuts saturated the air. The surf conditions were ideal, with cloudless blue skies and clear, warm water. Only a slight breeze blew down the valley, barely making the coconut fronds sway. This was a day of days for surfing.

I had been out since dawn and had caught some super waves. My rides had been exciting, and I was almost ready to quit, but it was hard to stop. Instead of going home to do some carpentry, I decided to paddle out for just one more wave. The surf had been eight to ten feet, but suddenly—and typically for Makaha—the waves jumped up to twelve to fourteen feet. A bit scary, but the conditions were perfect.

I wondered if I was up to this. My heart pounded as I headed a half mile out through the channel toward the point. All I could see were giant mounds of water forming lines on the horizon, moving in.

After what seemed like an endless paddle, I finally reached the lineup: the place where I wanted to sit and wait. I figured this could be a chance to catch the biggest wave of the set yet. The first wave approached, and I paddled as hard as possible to catch it—always the safest thing before the bigger and bigger waves roll in behind. I caught the wave with an exhilarating, steep drop of at least ten feet. This ride was like nothing I had experienced before, my best ride ever. I was ecstatic, feeling very proud of myself sliding across the face of this wall of water. Then, a few seconds later, the wave crested and broke, the whitewater crashing over me with a wild jolt. The force flipped me off my board and engulfed me in water and foam. I was pushed under with a power that tossed me head over heels like a rag doll in a washing machine. I was held underwater for what seemed like an eternity. I was powerless—caught up by the ocean's strength. As I struggled to reach the surface and get my head above foam, I remembered the advice I had been given by fellow surfers, to "relax, stretch out your extremities, and make yourself as big as possible." This would make me pop up to the surface of the foamy abyss. If your body is tense and rigid, you stay under the water longer. I desperately needed a breath, but I tried my best to get limp and be as big as possible. Then, after what seemed like forever, I popped up to the surface and caught one little breath before the next wave broke—pushing me back under the whitewater once again. This happened over and over. I had nothing to hang on to for support—this was long before leashes. By now, my board was headed to shore. I was a strong swimmer but wondered if I would drown.

Finally, there was a lull between sets. The waves eased up, and I made my way to shore, less swimming than being pushed by the currents. I staggered out of the water, trying to time my exit between the fierce shore-break waves. I made it onto the dry sand with barely enough strength to crawl and collapsed in sheer exhaustion.

Lying there, slowly catching my breath, I felt my life racing before me. I looked out to the surf break and wondered, How did I get myself into this?

CHAPTER 1

THE FIRST WAVE (1954)

On July 6, 1954, my mother and I woke up, ate breakfast, and drove to the beach. The sun was out, and the water was glistening. The brownish-green peaks of Diamond Head loomed on our left, and the pink, six-story splendor known as the Royal Hawaiian Hotel sat on our right. In front of the Outrigger Canoe Club, six-man canoes caught low breaking waves that rolled in toward shore. The ocean was sprinkled with people swimming and surfing. We put our beach bags on the sand and plunked down on our beach towels close to Charlie Amalu's station, where the beach boy had told my mother to meet him.

After a few minutes, my mother looked left toward the Moana Hotel and said, "Here he comes." She jumped up and walked toward the water's edge, greeting him joyfully. My sister, Gloria, and I followed hesitantly. When we reached the beach boy, my mother said, "Girls, I want you to meet Charlie. He's going to take us out in a canoe." We greeted him shyly but were eager to entrust ourselves to him.

The brown-skinned and muscular Charlie Amalu was friendly and elegant in an old-school Hawaiian way. He wore the beach boy uniform, a yellow tank top with navy blue shorts, along with a white baseball hat emblazoned with the red Outrigger Canoe Club emblem. Charlie's chiseled face and his sunny smile were endearing, if not irresistible, and Betty was immediately attracted. This might explain why she had arranged for Charlie to take us out in a canoe and introduce us to wave riding.

Charlie directed us toward a six-man canoe. Single- and double-hulled Hawaiian canoes are carved from the trunk of an aged-in-mud koa tree and have been a crucial part of Hawaiian voyaging, travel, and fishing. The canoe has two lateral support floats, called i'ako, attached to the hull with braided cords and to a horizontal boom called an ama.

Some beach boys pushed the canoe to the water's edge, and we three stepped in next to two other tourists already seated. After some "how to paddle" instruction, we made our way about a quarter mile out to where the waves were breaking. Charlie, the steersman, sat in the sixth seat at the back of the canoe. We arrived at the right spot to catch a wave; Charlie turned the canoe around and headed it toward shore. We sat there for a few minutes, waiting for a set of waves, before Charlie yelled, "Paddle! Paddle as hard as you can!" We grunted, dug in, pulled, caught the wave, and glided along the foamy crest as salt water sprayed across our faces. Then we caught several more, each as exciting as the last.

My mother had been taking in the surfers who were riding on the same wave with us. When we reached shore, she turned to Charlie and said, "I think I'd like to try surfing."

"Okay," he said, "how about a surf lesson?"

"Great! Let's go."

"Are you girls ready?" he asked.

Gloria and I gulped and eked out timid yeses. Charlie walked deliberately to his station and chose three surfboards. He carried them to the water's edge and assigned one to each of us. Gloria was nine, and I was thirteen. We were both fairly obedient girls. We hesitated, then realized we had better summon our bravest selves. Our mother displayed no such hesitations.

"Lie down on your board," Charlie said, "and I'll show you how to paddle and stand up once I push you into a wave." Stretched out on the boards, still perched on the sand, we pretended to dig our skinny arms into water, mimicking him. My mother followed suit. He then picked up his board and said, "Follow me." Charlie led us to the water, lay on his board, and started paddling out to where the waves were breaking. Dutifully, we followed.

The surf break stretching in front of the Moana Hotel is known as Canoes. Charlie stopped at the first inner break, an excellent spot for beginners. He got off his board and turned it around to face the shore. We did the same. Here, the water was just above waist deep. Charlie said, "Gloria, you can be first." Gloria lay on her board and got ready to catch her wave. When it came, Charlie gave her a big push. She stood up and rode the wave toward shore.

"Vicky, you're next." I waited for the next wave, my wave. When it came close, I plunged my arms into the water, taking a few strokes, before Charlie propelled me. I caught the wave and stood up for a minute or so, before falling off. The top of my leg hit the board. It hurt like heck, so painful that I didn't want to go back for any more, but my troupe was out there waiting. As I paddled nervously back out, I heard Charlie say, "Mom, this one is for you." He pushed Betty into the wave and yelled, "Stand up, Mom." I watched my mother catch her wave, stand up, and ride joyfully all the way to shore. She came back out with a big smile on her face. I could see she was hooked.

For the rest of the summer, my mother was at the beach every morning and surfing every day, trying hard to improve her skills. Surely, Charlie Amalu had something to do with her passion. But, as I had seen her do with other pursuits in her life, she worked.

Surfing for me was not love at first try, but over the next weeks my mother talked me into going back out with her. Gradually, I, too, became addicted. Gloria was less interested. She didn't like being held under the water by a wave and thought there were too many surfers competing for rides. Soon she said, "No more."

Betty was forty-one when she started surfing at Waikiki. It liberated her in more ways than one. Sometimes she surfed alongside Charlie, but she was also meeting new people. She was gaining physical and psychological strength. She was experiencing nature and her own place in it. She was, as we were all learning to say, "stoked."

We returned home to Chino from our summer vacation, and, though I didn't witness it, my mother began a heavy lobbying campaign.

My father himself visited Oahu several weeks later. He could not fathom our infatuation.

Gloria and I counted the days till we could get back to Hawaii. My mother had vowed to return the day after Christmas 1954. At that time, Hawaii was still a territory. Dwight Eisenhower was president of the United States. Mass vaccination of children against polio had just begun, and Elvis Presley cut his first commercial record. The beatnik movement was on the horizon, amid an anti-materialist and counter-culture rebellion. More housewives were moving into the workplace, but divorce was uncommon. It was still a conservative time for women. But my mother was feeling an independence that had characterized her younger years.

CHAPTER 2

PIONEER ORIGINS (1913–29)

Born Elizabeth Pembroke in Salt Lake City, Utah, on June 5, 1913, Betty was the second of six siblings. Her sister Jane was older by two years, and she had four younger siblings: Catherine, Herbert, Ann, and Patricia. Patricia, though, died at eighteen months.

The family patriarch, Earl Richard Pembroke, was an independent man who was fascinated with the mountains and the riches they held. He attended MIT before graduating from Columbia's School of Mines in 1903 with a mining engineering degree. He had a wiry but strong five-foot-seven build and was an oarsman on the college rowing team, a track-and-field runner, and an outdoor adventurer. Philosophical, with high ideals, Earl was also down to earth. After college, he worked for a mining company and soon thrived financially.

The family matriarch, Violet Elizabeth Rule, was of French Canadian descent and grew up on a dairy farm near Spokane, Washington. Elizabeth was a couple inches taller than Earl, with a fleshy body and longish brown hair that she kept pulled back off her face. Elizabeth was elegant, determined, and dignified. After high school, she studied nursing at Sacred Hearts College in Washington and planned to study surgical nursing at Johns Hopkins University. But during a summer job after

5

college in Salt Lake City, she met Earl Pembroke. They courted. Elizabeth gave up her studies and happily married in 1910, into a more prestigious station. Aristocratic airs seemed to come naturally to her. Family members often referred to her as the Duchess.

Elizabeth Violet Pembroke

Yet Elizabeth was a strong-willed, no-nonsense woman—she was an early female automobile driver in Salt Lake City and acted briefly in local Shakespearean plays, and at home she was a strict disciplinarian, demanding good manners and obedient behavior. Her children were all a little frightened of her and also wanted to please her; they tried their best to behave when in her company. Her granddaughter Jamie remembers her as "rarely cuddly."

In the teens and early 1920s, the Pembroke family lived in what was known in Salt Lake as a "dear old adobe," called Rosebank Cottage. Brigham Young gave Robert Dye, who had traveled to Salt Lake with the John Young party in 1847, the property in 1870. At age thirty, Dye was already a plant enthusiast and lived in a tent while he landscaped the garden, helping Brigham Young fulfill his promise to "make the desert bloom like a rose." Dye planted numerous imported varieties of trees and flowering plants. The summer garden became a well-known attraction for early visitors to the city.

Earl's mother, Sarah Jane Pembroke, had bought the landmark in 1903 and lived there until 1918, when she moved out and her son and his family moved in. As a child, Betty had spent precious time at the cottage with her grandmother, and she adored its little rooms and the garden.

"The walls were thick enough to withstand an invading army, with deep window ledges and two funny little fireplaces that threw out an incredible amount of heat," Betty wrote when she was twenty-four. "Warm in the winter and delightfully cool in the hot summers, Rosebank Cottage had an ornate, black, wrought-iron fence around the front yard shielding it from the sidewalk."

"The garden was a joy to a small adventurer," wrote the young Betty. An English Hawthorne produced pink blossoms each June. A Norwegian maple generated tan winged pods that flew in whirls in the fall winds. A garden swing hung from a giant mulberry tree. A luncheon table and playhouse sat under an umbrella tree whose sheltering branches softened the summer sun. A catalpa tree leaned over the cottage protectively, and a high hedge provided privacy. Peach and myrtle trees completed the garden, as well as flower beds that contained nasturtiums and sunflowers. "Roses of all varieties and colors filled the air with fragrance," Betty wrote.

Though Betty waxed on about the smells and sights of the garden in her writing, she was hardly a mere spectator in life. When she was as young as three, her father noticed her manual dexterity and her inventive urge. She wrote that he described her as "skilled at doing things with her hands and intent on creating small objects." Wanting to nurture this gift, Earl bought Betty a "complete tool chest in miniature size and kept her supplied with craft and building materials when she expressed a desire for them." In her "tool kit," Betty wrote years later, "were putty, cement, nails, leather, glue, glass, rope, and wire." By the age of ten, she had learned to carve or build miniature characters, animals, and objects.

Rambunctious Play

After moving into Rosebank Cottage, Earl continued to find financial success in the mining business. He and Elizabeth wanted a larger and more elegant home, and in 1926, when Betty was thirteen, the Pembrokes moved to a three-story house at 666 East South Temple Street, in an area known as the 20th Ward or the Avenues. In 1856, Brigham Young had staked out and surveyed this region, previously owned by the federal government. The Mormon leader used the land to fulfill his promise of property and better days for his Mormon recruits, doling out the parcels for $2.50, the cost of the paperwork. By the early 1900s, artists, writers, actors, musicians, politicians, and the elite of early Salt Lake City lived on the Avenues.

The Pembrokes' house was located a few houses away from that of Utah's governor, George Dern, whose reign lasted from 1925 to 1933. (Later, Dern became secretary of war under Franklin D. Roosevelt.) Before he was elected governor, the non-Mormon Dern had been vice president of the Mercur Gold Mining Company, where he coinvented the Holt-Dern ore-roasting process, a technique for recovering silver from low-grade ores. He and Earl shared a passion for mining. Earl and Elizabeth, now prosperous young socialites, became part of the Derns' inner circle. The Derns hosted elaborate parties, entertaining guests who included political dignitaries and business friends. The Pembrokes soon followed suit.

Betty adored her daredevil play with the neighborhood children. She jumped off rooftops into banks of snow and ran wild through the stately avenues. During the long Salt Lake winters, she often played in the Derns' three-story Victorian, known as the Conklin-Dern Mansion. The house had three fireplaces with corresponding steeples, as well as exquisite chandeliers and stained-glass windows. Unlike in the Pembroke family, the children were given permission to roam throughout the house, where, according to a contemporary description, "each room was dressed in its own fine woodwork panels of cherry, mahogany, walnut, maple, and oak." Betty loved best the hide-and-seek they played in the darkly lit rooms, including a third-story ballroom converted into a billiards room.

On special occasions when Betty was a teen, Earl drove the older children up to the Park City and Bingham Mines, where he often worked, and where Betty greeted the miners and explored the dark mine shafts. The family also occasionally traveled to Elizabeth's parents' dairy farm in Idaho, where, at age twelve, Betty played in the open spaces with farm equipment and a car for pretend driving. She was fascinated with cars, and at home, before she was old enough to drive on the streets, she spent time maneuvering the family Studebaker up and down the driveway. (Eventually the girls would drive it to school.)

Betty behind the wheel in Idaho on grandparent's dairy farm

Elizabeth suffered from allergies, so each March she left Salt Lake before the trees started spreading pollen. When the children were in grade school, she packed them up and took them by train to California to attend school for the remaining three or four months of the school year. Betty was, she later wrote, "deliriously happy" in Santa Monica. Shortly after returning home to Salt Lake, the family would leave for camping in the nearby mountains or Yellowstone National Park. This was when Betty learned to make a campfire and cook over open coals.

Betty described her childhood as joyous; she had fond memories of those summer travels and a special trip, at age ten, to San Francisco. Elizabeth led the children through Chinatown and into shops where she bought them lychee fruit, sugared walnuts, candied watermelon rind and ginger, dolls, and little white Chinese bowls decorated with blue carp. They also crossed town to the wharf to watch fishermen bring in live crabs and lobsters and then cook them in big black pots on the sidewalk. The children carried home parcels of seafood for supper, along with long loaves of sourdough bread and red wine in bottle baskets. Jane, Betty, Catherine, Herbert, and Ann were allowed to sip the wine, and they drank in the novelty of such outings.

Betty wrote about one excursion through Golden Gate Park. At the Japanese garden, they drank tea and ate rice cookies. They sailed little boats on a small lake and used bows and arrows at a target range. Another highlight was gathering poppies in the field on the hill overlooking the Sutro gardens, with their small sculptures from Dickens novels. These statues of Tiny Tim and Mr. Pickwick may have been the first expression of Betty's lifelong fascination with miniature figures.

Grandmother Pem, as we grandchildren knew her, placed a high value on how a person looked. This is not surprising, as her father was said to be a dandy. She believed in feminine attire for girls and women and tried to groom her daughters accordingly. "One never knows if one will meet her next husband at the market," she would say. "Always look your best." Most important, she told her daughters, "Remember that you are a Pembroke and you must behave like one." Grandmother Pem's Victorian propriety often veered into snobbery. She was class-conscious, keeping close track of the affluence and education of others.

Betty, though, was humble and unpretentious. She had a stronger connection with her mining engineer father than she did with her striving mother, yet she fretted over how to please Elizabeth. In spite of Betty's striking looks—she had a strong, triangle-shaped nose and high cheekbones, greenish-blue eyes, chestnut brown hair, and smooth skin—she grew up feeling like the family's ugly duckling. She was a tomboy, a natural athlete, and, most of all, a fierce competitor.

This may partly explain her special bond with her younger brother, although Herbert's childhood was even more complicated than his sister's. When he was five years old, Herbert went for a swim in the municipal pool and caught spinal meningitis, an acute inflammation of the protective membranes covering the brain and spinal cord. He was bedridden for several months, lost his hearing, and remained deaf for the rest of his life. With the help of his mother and a tutor, he learned to read lips and became a proficient communicator. Betty, then twelve years old, looked out for him as if he were her own child.

A couple of years later, on July 4, 1927, another disaster struck one of the siblings. A rogue firecracker set older sister Jane's dress on fire, and Jane went running off before anyone could wrap her in a blanket to extinguish the flames. The sixteen-year-old spent a year in recovery and ended up with ugly scarring on her arm and torso. She also missed a year of school. As a result, Betty and Jane ended up in the same high school class. The accident may have changed Jane's body, but it didn't alter her essential disposition. Jane was a debutante (she came out to society in Salt Lake City), and she, Catherine, and Ann all followed their mother's model, happily immersing themselves in social activities that Betty cared nothing for.

In fact, Betty dreamed of having a career so she could be independent from the kind of domestic world her mother endorsed. She had already been advanced in school, but she worked overtime at her studies, driven by an intense determination to be successful and to, as she put it, "have a profession."

During her teenage years, Betty was attracted to some of the neighborhood boys, but she was more drawn to horseback riding, tennis, roller skating, ice skating, and skiing in the foothills of the Wasatch Mountains. This was before ski lifts; the teenagers climbed up the mountain, sidestepping one foot at a time. The precious reward was only one or two ski runs down, as it took the better part of the day to reach the top.

Strong and tall for her age, Betty made competitive play a top priority; track-and-field events particularly suited her. She liked winning the gold medal and shrugged off the silver or bronze. She was voted Best

Athlete for hurdles and track during her senior year in high school and kept the trophy her entire life.

Betty liked to show off her muscles, Hercules-style, and even liked arm wrestling, especially when she beat the boys. She continued arm wrestling well into her midseventies, challenging both women and men friends at social gatherings.

Losing the House

Betty spent her first fifteen years in what she called a "luxuriously happy and carefree life." Then the kind of financial disaster that would soon grip the nation hit her family hard. Earl had taken his mining wealth and invested overconfidently in the stock market. He leveraged his investments and bought mining stock on the short margin. In February 1929, eight months before the bottom fell out of the stock market in the Great Crash, Earl lacked adequate cash to back up his marginal investments. He lost everything.

Betty was home with her family one evening when they heard a knock. Elizabeth opened the door; three men stood outside and announced that they had come to remove the house furnishings. Everything would be auctioned to pay off Earl's stock market debt. The family watched with disbelief as the men carried out the Pembroke antiques: two pianos, artwork, sofas, chairs, lamps, tables, beds, and dressers. The entire contents of their house on the Avenues were loaded into several trucks and taken away. They never saw their belongings again.

Throughout her life, Betty told the story of watching the family's household (especially her bedroom furniture) being hauled off. "The memory of this event was as vivid as on the day it happened," she said. The shock and disappointment shaped her attitude about money and spending. She vowed to live a careful life so that financial ruin would never come again to her or her family. Until she was ninety-eight, Betty used cash for most all purchases and ardently saved for an increasingly distant "rainy day."

After the humiliation of the stock market debacle and the loss of their home, the family moved into a hotel to regroup. Betty, Jane, and

Catherine had been day students at Saint-Mary-of-the-Wasatch, a finishing school in Salt Lake City. In short order, they became boarding students. The Catholic Sisters of the Holy Cross ran the school with an iron hand. In spite of the rigorous standards, Betty, now in her senior year, was a good student in Spanish, Latin, English, mathematics, dramatics, physics, secretarial work, and chemistry. (There was also athletic training.) The three Pembroke sisters lived in one room and shared a bath with two other girls. Fooling around was not tolerated; they had to settle down to earnest study. Betty thrived in the peaceful atmosphere the nuns established for boarders, quite the opposite of the more raucous setting she had known on the Avenues.

Life was regimented, but Betty later noted that the sisters managed to have fun on their nightly adventures while the watchful nuns were sleeping. They took joy from middle-of-the-night "banquets" at which they secretly feasted on sardines, crackers, and cheese in the bathroom, and they occasionally carried their bedclothes and mattresses up to the finely graveled rooftop to sleep under the spell of the moon.

CHAPTER 3

CALIFORNIA DREAMING (1929–36)

Within months of losing their home, in the spring of 1929, Earl and Elizabeth moved with seven-year-old Herbert and five-year-old Ann to Santa Monica. Earl went to work for an oil company in San Pedro.

The three older girls remained in boarding school in Salt Lake City. Despite having her sisters as roommates, Betty missed the rest of her family and suffered from loneliness. An immature high school senior (she was, after all, still only fifteen), she had trouble adjusting to the separation from her parents. And as she had been a surrogate mother to Herbert, she pined for her younger brother. Herbert wrote sweet letters telling her how much he missed her and detailing his daily activities. One of these letters, written on his personalized stationery, was sent in March 1929.

Dear Betty Pembroke,

The letter you sent me was very good. I miss you so so much. I am a good boy in school and the teacher says I will be in fifth grade next year. My teeth are strong and I brush them everyday [sic]. I have a piece of gold to send you.

Bybyby, I love you,
Herbert Earl Pembroke

Herbert grew into a lanky, strong, and handsome young man. He worked his way through Cal Poly College with a degree in animal husbandry, became a farrier and then a cowboy.

Betty turned sixteen on June 5, 1929, and she and Jane graduated that same month. (Jane had returned to school after her year's convalescence and joined Betty's class.) Then Jane, Betty, and Catherine, now often called Cay, traveled to Santa Monica on the train with their grandparents to join the rest of the family.

That first summer along the Pacific Ocean was a memorable time for Betty. She spent every day at the beach, body-surfing the top-to-bottom-breaking big combers and swimming around the piers. She became a strong swimmer and competed in various rough-water swims in Santa Monica.

Betty took to beach life naturally and got to know various lifeguards, many of whom were the great watermen of the day. Pete Peterson, an early California surfer, invited her to paddle with him on his large, hollow racing board. This was Betty's first time on a surfboard, and she was exhilarated, even if they didn't catch any waves.

Betty was sixteen, and she considered herself lucky. She had had a life of intense, constant play, whether racing through the Derns' mansion, throwing herself into games in spelling class, or skating after school. Now she was completely in her element. She later wrote that she would never be "entirely played out." Her thirst for sport would indeed never be slaked, but an appetite for work complemented it. To her, play and work were not mutually exclusive.

Dominant Aspirations

In Santa Monica, even as she raced around piers, body-surfing the Pacific combers, Betty contemplated a future in which she would be self-supporting. During the summer of 1929, through her parents, she met a dentist who promised her a job working in dental hygiene if she were to enter that field. Betty jumped at this opportunity. She applied and was accepted to the University of Southern California's dental hygiene program, where she immediately started a two-year course. To be near school, she moved from Santa Monica to Los Angeles and lived with family friends, Margaret and Frank Strong, whom she affectionately called Aunt Margaret and Uncle Frank.

Betty loved dental school and appreciated her new cohort. Though she was only sixteen and a good bit younger than her classmates, she was a serious student, spending long hours with her books. On occasional weekends, she and her friends went to the beach at Santa Monica. Sometimes they ventured farther afield, and Betty started to have an appreciation for people with life stories different from her own.

In 1930, five of the girls drove up north for the USC–UC Berkeley football game. One of the classmates was black. When the girls arrived at their hotel, the receptionist said, "We don't let black people stay here." She said Betty's friend would have to go down the street to another hotel. Betty had long had a mutual admiration with her black nanny, who had worked in the Pembroke home and helped raise the children. She considered herself color-blind, but she came to realize that this perception might be naive. At that moment in Berkeley, feeling bad for her friend, she said, "Okay, I'll go with you and stay there also." Off they walked to the other hotel. There she met another surprise. The reservationist said, "Sorry, but we don't let white people stay here." Betty argued but soon figured there was no use. She walked back and joined the three other white girls, and her black friend had to stay alone.

The incident stayed with her and shaped her attitude in the years to come.

"I was born on June 5, on a Thursday," Betty would one day write, reflecting on the adage that "Wednesday's child was loving and giving, but Thursday's child was born to work." To her, work was play—it was a new challenge, and every challenge was fun.

Dental hygiene was a brand-new profession, and in 1932 Betty was in the second class to graduate from the University of Southern California. She held license number 119 in the state. (For the next fifty years, she renewed this license and kept it current—just in case.) Dental college awakened her. "Childish dreams were shattered," she later wrote about that time.

Betty Pembroke University of Southern California Graduation, 1932

"Life assumed a new color when so many responsibilities were placed on my shoulders." She was just nineteen years old when she graduated, and she marveled that it put her in a position to render a health service to others. She believed that destiny had led her into this field and that she had an obligation to do the right thing.

At twenty-three, she typed out a credo that seemed to inspire her for years to come:

> *You are today where your thoughts have brought you.*
> *You will be tomorrow where your thoughts have taken you.*
> *You cannot escape the results of your thoughts*
> *Be they base, beautiful, or a mixture of both,*
> *For you will always gravitate toward that which you secretly most love.*
> *Whatever your present environment might be*
> *You will rise, remain, or fall,*
> *According to your ambitions, your ideals.*
> *You will become as small as your controlling desire,*
> *Or as great as your dominant aspiration.*

After graduation in 1932, Betty moved back to Santa Monica to work for the dentist who had promised to hire her. A few months later, at nineteen, she began a succession of jobs for several different dentists. Unfortunately, not all dentists or patients took seriously such a young woman. For the first few years, Betty worked extra hard to prove that she was a qualified hygienist, competent and capable of taking superior care of patients.

In this, she had the unwavering support of her father, with whom she had always enjoyed a deep sympathy. On May 5, 1932, Earl sent his daughter a letter that reveals a certain tenderness, as well as paternal pride in a daughter who shared his drive and his philosophical bent. Curiously, the letter has him looking to the sea for answers to existential questions.

Greenville.
Plumas Co., Calif.
May 5, 1932

Dear Betty:

Have your letter without date today. We are very glad your hard year's work is soon to be over and you have a little rest but, more important, a little change. You have done WELL, my dear, and we are more than proud of you.

Do not think you have to learn everything right now; the trail is rather a long, hard one, and if you will maintain your interest in the absorption of the knowledge, which is the accumulated experience of mankind, you find at your hand a (THE) great source of pleasure. Keep up your Spanish by all means. You can do that by talking and reading diligently a good little weekly paper or magazine printed in Spanish. Think there must be some such thereabouts.

Uncle Frank and Aunt Margaret have done a marvelous thing for your Mother and Dad—and that means for you. LOVE, in its many ramifications and manifestations, is THE MOTIVATING INFLUENCE of LIFE.

I told you a long time ago that we came from the sea—from "Fish," using the word in a general sense. The first life cell I believe developed in water, and it is conceivable that in the beginning of existence of water on Earth there were several or many varieties of water— that is, in the mineral varieties and contents of the waters of the earth. When you stop to consider the infinite variety of conditions existing in the sea or seas that that first poor little life cell must needs successfully combat, perhaps you can picture the development of a great family of sea urchins that had in the meantime developed the five senses one at a time and perhaps in the order of Feel, Taste,

Smell, Hear, and See. I believe each variety of this large family of sea urchins was decided way back in the dim past by the conditions surrounding and guiding, and causing emergences—and perhaps even earlier.

You see what your question started? You can spend many interesting and profitable hours in reading and speculating on the possibilities of the great development of life's manifestations on Earth. It is a subject of intense interest, and will bring you up to a fundamental understanding of modern psychology, and better still, if you reflect upon it properly and contemporaneously, it will give you a more complete understanding of Human Nature, and as THAT is what you must contact in practically every waking hour, it will help you to live more successfully and happily with other human beings—and that is the great job in life.

Your Dad did not start these studies early enough in life to have received the full benefit—I mean a benefit to be derived from a more complete understanding, from a spirit of tolerance. But we will get there yet, my dear. Just try to do your best, have courage always, NEVER FEEL INFERIOR, be honest at ALL times, be just, and keep busy. You know now a large part of your Dad's philosophy of life. If you can be and do these things, adding sympathy and kindness, you will develop a character that will sustain you through any adversity, when and if it comes.

Our love to you all. Mother has not been feeling very well for a few days. Weather here has been BAD—wet and cold, and infection got from the throat (or rather nasal cavity) into that crooked old canal to the ear. Better today.

Say hello to Dr. Mike. I wrote him.

Yours,
Dad

Betty and Earl Pembroke at USC graduation

Betty thrived on her father's attention. She was driven to excellence, and throughout her life she indulged her own curiosity in a way that would have pleased him. But in 1932 she was also driven by exigency. Earl Pembroke never fully recovered from his losses before and during the Depression, and his three oldest daughters were left to their own devices. Betty was supporting herself and her two sisters. Jobs were scarce, and Cay and Jane were less educated and ambitious than she was. After Betty paid the rent, there was little extra money to buy food. Carrots at five cents a bag were her staple. Considered the beauties of the family, Cay and Jane were glamorous and popular. They dated and snuck food home for their older sister, waking Betty up when they returned with leftovers. She depended on them for food, and they depended on her for a place to live.

Driven to Adventure

As thrilled as she was with her new career, Betty never stopped filling her off-hours. She rode horses and played tennis. Despite her diet of carrots, she continually entered rough-water ocean swims in Santa Monica, winning and placing in several events. She was noticed and invited to swim at an exclusive polo club, the Uplifters. Located on 120 wooded acres in Rustic Canyon, the Uplifters was where she first started serious training. Some friends admired her strength and swimming style and suggested she try out for the swim team at the Los Angeles Athletic Club.

Located on Seventh Street in downtown LA, the Los Angeles Athletic Club was founded in 1880, when the city had only eleven-thousand residents. After the Depression, the private club did a one-time merger with several other Southern California clubs in preparation for the 1932 Los Angeles Olympics. The merger gave members the advantages of five clubs for the price of one—the "allied clubs." Duke Kahanamoku swam for the club in its early years, but the victories in the 1924, 1928, and 1932 Olympics raised its prominence; Buster Crabbe, Johnny Weissmuller, Mickey Riley, and Walter Spence all claimed medals and congregated at the club. In 1933, when Betty tried out, the Los Angeles Athletic Club was *the* place to swim. She made the team and started a vigorous training program, with the goal of swimming the freestyle event at the Berlin Olympics in 1936. For several years, she commuted to Los Angeles after work, training every night for two to three hours in the indoor "plunge," which was thirty-two by one hundred feet. Betty was introduced to a popular swim coach, Henry O'Byrne, a man who had seen her compete in and win rough-water swims in Santa Monica. He thought Betty would be another Helene Madison, the three-time gold-medal winner in the 1932 Los Angeles Olympics. Betty kept up her rigorous schedule, but, after a few months of training, Coach O'Byrne was killed in an auto accident. Betty was devastated; O'Byrne's death almost ended her swimming career. Never one to give up, though, she kept her sights on the Olympics.

A better-paying job presented itself with a dentist who had an upscale practice with film people. Betty was now taking care of and getting to know patients who were cameramen, stuntmen, makeup artists, and Hollywood stars, such as Gloria Swanson. (Betty later named her second daughter after the screen star.) The great tap dancer Bill "Bojangles" Robinson was another patient. He told her that if she ever had a son, he would teach him to dance; if she had girls, he warned, she was out of luck. (After working with Shirley Temple, he had sworn he would not teach any more girls.)

Betty scraped up enough money to take flying lessons from a friend of a dental patient. She had long been fascinated with flying and read books as a child about the Wright Brothers. Amelia Earhart, Betty's kind of adventurer, had made her solo transatlantic flight in 1932, and newspapers and radio had followed her exploits. By age twenty-two, in 1935, Betty had accumulated eight hours of flight instruction in a single-engine Waco airplane and had earned her student pilot's license.

Betty with her flight instructor in front of Waco Plane, 1936

Soon, another dental patient, who was a friend of Gus Briegleb, the noted glider builder and flier, invited Betty to go out and see Briegleb flying at the old Los Angeles Municipal Mines Field annex. She drove out to the flying field, watched the show, and met Briegleb. Glider flying is the closest man can come to being a bird, Briegleb told her. Betty was smitten. She had always been entranced by birds and their ability to "take to the air."

Gus Briegleb invited her to try out his glider. Eager to start flying on her own, yet with only eight hours of flying lessons in the single-engine Waco, she talked the flight instructor into letting her solo in the glider. The only instruction she remembered his giving her was that she was not to land in the Japanese farmers' vegetable gardens across the highway.

She agreed and got in. The guys towed her down the takeoff/landing strip. She took to the air and, at the appropriate height, released the cable attached to the car. She was soaring on her own, gliding free as a bird above the Los Angeles airport area. After five or ten minutes, she nosed down slightly in order to gain speed to get over some high-tension power lines looming ahead. Suddenly, the glider went into an irretrievable spin and nosedived into the ground from sixty-five feet. The force of impact shoved Betty's body forward and pushed her leg against the bent girder of the plane, breaking her right limb in a compound fracture.

Several people rushed out and lifted her from the wreckage. They called an ambulance and loaded Betty onto the gurney; a friend jumped in beside her. But she hadn't been properly strapped in. As the driver took off, he rounded a corner too fast and Betty slid off the gurney and onto the floor of the ambulance. The driver told her friend, "She had better stretch that leg out straight, or she could be a cripple for life." Betty remembered being conscious all the way to the hospital, but in shock. She also remembered telling the ambulance driver that he was not to say a word to her mother about the crash.

Wounds Confine Glider Aviatrix

Ambitions of Betty Pembroke, 23-year-old aviatrix, to become a glider as well as airplane pilot, but who crashed in the attempt, faded yesterday when she learned her injuries will keep her on the ground for the next few months.

The girl, who resides at 1181 Victoria avenue, suffered a broken leg and concussion of the brain Sunday when her motorless craft crashed to the ground from an altitude of fifty feet near Mines Field. She is in Centinela Hospital, Inglewood.

Los Angeles Times article of
Betty's glider accident, 1936

After a time in the hospital, Elizabeth, although angered, nursed Betty back to health at home in Santa Monica. To Betty, the recovery from a compound fracture seemed an eternity. She hated being a semi-invalid, and she regretted being away from her office. After six weeks, she returned to work. Standing on her feet all day, cleaning teeth with a broken leg in a cast, was uncomfortable and tiring, but she needed the money. She persevered.

Elizabeth and Earl got over their fury at their daughter's having crashed Gus Briegleb's glider. Briegleb fixed the glider, and, despite the mishap, he and Betty parted as friends. The Department of Air Commerce was less forgiving and notified Betty that her license had been revoked.

Worse, her leg was in a cast for several months, and that dashed her Olympic dreams. The leg bothered her off and on for the rest of her life, but she never let the discomfort get in the way of her participation in other sports.

"It was a lucky break to survive that crash," Betty admitted. She came to believe that she had a guardian angel who protected her during her own risky adventures, her Waterloos.

CHAPTER 4

LOST WAX AND WHITE GOLD (1937–51)

Betty observed the dentists she worked for and conjured a new challenge. She loved being a dental hygienist, but why not be a dentist? She entered night school at her alma mater, the University of Southern California, to start the prerequisite classes.

There, she befriended Grace Griffin, a USC librarian. Grace arranged an introduction to her brother, Ronald Heldreich. Ron and Betty met and hit it off. Ron was a manufacturing jeweler making rings, necklaces, and earrings, and he could fix anything. On the weekends, Ron dove for the glass-bottom boat on Catalina Island, searching for underwater treasures while tourists looked on. Betty fell in love. The two shared a creative spirit, a love for the ocean, and a lust for the new. They eloped to Mexico in May 1937, having known each other for only a few weeks.

Ron, my father, was thirty-seven years old, twelve years older than Betty, and a handsome smooth talker. Born in England, he had come to America with his mother and father when he was one. He had two younger sisters, Grace and Millie, and a brother, Harry.

His parents, Ada and Harry, were first cousins. Ada adored her oldest child. She called him her "golden boy." The siblings knew he was her favorite. Maybe this led to his thinking he could make up tales with impunity. (When I was a teenager, my mother told me my father "would climb a tree to tell an untrue story.")

My father and his siblings all shared temperamental personalities; they became angered by or upset with each other easily and often. They couldn't sit down for a meal together without someone making trouble. One family member would be pitted against another for the rest of their lives.

Shortly after returning from Mexico, Betty wrote to Earl, announcing her marriage with a glowing report about the wonders of Ron Heldreich. Curiously, she added that if it didn't work, she would chalk it up to experience. Before putting the letter in a drawer, Earl added a cryptic note in the margin: "Nice letter anyway." In fact, both parents disapproved.

Betty had led a sheltered life and was naive. She was attracted to men, and men liked her, but she had had no boyfriends or romances in high school or college; her career, athletics, and education were more important. Ron was her first love.

A year later, Betty wrote in her journal, "I always claimed I would never marry, but out of the teeming fullness of the earth came the man of my subconscious ideals. He swept me off my feet, and my adventurous and impetuous soul leaped into a life for which it was not suited."

Ron had promised to help Betty become a dentist, but he proved to be unserious. Betty's first stumbling block was organic chemistry. She took it two times but could not get the required B grade. Ron couldn't help her with Organic Chemistry and neither of them knew to turn to tutors or mentors. Betty had the necessary manual dexterity, strong work ethic, likable personality, and love of dentistry, but instead of offering moral (or financial) support, Ron suggested she help him part-time with his own jewelry business.

Betty gave up on dental school. She worked as a hygienist and learned the jewelry business in her spare time. She was happy, though, to take up jewelry making. "I have always felt the urge to work with my hands, to carve objects in wax and cast them in silver and gold," she wrote in her autobiography, noting that in dental school, making tiny elephants and rings had become a hobby. She could look at an animal or figure and replicate it in miniature, creating a charm, pendant, or ring. It took a few years, though, before she worked full-time with my father.

Palos Verdes

Shortly after they got married, Betty and Ron moved from Los Angeles to Palos Verdes. Originally a Spanish land grant called Rancho Palos Verdes, the area is a peninsula rising 1,400 feet above the ocean, situated between the South Bay of metropolitan Los Angeles and San Pedro, farther to the south. In the early 1920s and '30s, it was an area of dusty, rolling hills covered only with a scattering of trees and coastal sage. Developers chose a section called Portuguese Bend as the first site for housing, as it had a consistently mild, fog-free climate. It was a natural water playground, with tide pools and caves lining the beach.

In 1913, Frank Vanderlip had purchased the sixteen-thousand-acre property sight unseen. The New York banker said the description reminded him of Italy, where he regularly vacationed. Vanderlip and a consortium of New York investors envisioned an Italian hillside village occupied by two hundred craftsmen who lived, worked, and sold their wares. Additional plans included a golf course, swimming pool, riding club, and tennis courts.

The Vanderlip estate sat on the cliff just above the beach. The dry hills were home to grazing sheep and cattle. Japanese families farmed vegetables on small patches of rented land. Rows of cypress trees lined the driveways and a path to the beach. Through a grove of mature eucalyptus trees was an expansive view of twenty-six-mile-long Catalina Island, located twenty miles offshore.

Betty and Ron settled into the Gatehouse, also known as Villa Palos Verdes, a cottage at the entrance to the Vanderlip estate. It and a house named Villa Narcissa were the first two of the four buildings on the property. The Mediterranean-style villas each had thick pink stucco walls joined by arches and rust-brown tile roofs. Brick paths circled around gardens with short hedges that formed borders for rose gardens and led to a central courtyard with a fountain.

The Gatehouse was modeled after the sixteenth-century roadside chapel that Michelangelo occupied when he painted the ceiling of the

Sistine Chapel. The villa even has a room off the entrance designed as a chapel with a twenty-foot high-beamed ceiling. (Today the Gatehouse is home to the Portuguese Bend Art Colony and on the National Register of Historic Places.)

In 1929, after four of the villas were built, the Depression interrupted the development plan. When my parents moved from Los Angeles into the Gatehouse cottage in the late 1930s, Vanderlip's dream had stalled out, but Ron and Betty were able to, in a way, live his vision.

Ron and Betty thought one of the best features of their new home was the beach, Abalone Cove, just a five-minute stroll down the hill. The water teemed with fish, abalone, and lobsters. Ron worked as a civilian for the Navy, and Betty worked as a hygienist. Weekends were filled with swimming, diving, sunbathing, and fishing.

Vanderlip beach clubhouse at Abaloni Cove, Palos Verdes California
Siblings: Herbert, Catherine, Betty, and Jane Pembroke

They bought a twenty-three-foot sailboat, *Vagabond*, and Betty learned to pilot it. They occasionally sailed out to Catalina Island, where Ron dove for abalone. They moored *Vagabond* in Avalon Harbor and in the evenings would row ashore to the town of Avalon, with its renowned art deco revival casino. Decorated with sterling silver and gold-leaf accents, the casino had the world's largest circular ballroom, holding three thousand dancers, who dined and danced to "sweet jazz" played by big-band notables such as Jan Garber, Kay Kyser, Russ Brown, and Guy Lombardo and His Royal Canadians. Life was romantic.

Even if Betty had admitted doubts in her journal about whether married life suited her, the first years with Ron defined the term "ignorance is bliss." They shared an artisanal business, a beach life, and a kind of deep commonality. Both their grandparents and their great-grandparents had been metal artists in eighteenth-century England; it was as though Betty and Ron were genetically bonded. But as time went on, the parity in their vocations and avocations was not enough to temper a disparity in their personalities. The gender-role conventions of the period probably only exacerbated their different expectations of life. Little by little, my father dominated my mother. Her life became subsumed in his.

A black-and-white photo taken at Catalina soon after they were married captures Ron and Betty as they have just come out of the water. Betty is twenty-five years old, with strong shoulders and a broad upper body. She wears a black one-piece bathing suit; her slightly curly hair is tucked under a white bathing cap. Her sculpted nose and high cheekbones stand out, as does her smile, with its ever-so-perfect teeth. Double-imposed over her image is a second image, of Ron. He is thirty-six years old. His pate is bald, his arms crossed over his bare, muscular torso. His steel-blue eyes gaze off into the distance.

After three years of marriage, my parents started a family. I was born on September 18, 1940, in Palos Verdes. Life there had continued to enthrall them, but soon the United States' conflict with Japan started heating up. My mother and her friends worried after they discovered a two-man Japanese submarine in a cave along their beach. Soon after that scare, the Japanese bombed Pearl Harbor. Two weeks later, the *Absaroka*, an American merchant ship carrying lumber, was torpedoed three hundred nautical miles off San Pedro. Japanese submarines were spotted patrolling off the California coast.

Fear took hold, given Palos Verdes' strategic proximity to the Los Angeles and San Pedro harbors. My father was recruited into the Navy as a lieutenant transportation officer at nearby Terminal Island. Then

Betty and Ron after a swim at Catalina, 1937

paranoia set in: A Japanese invasion was thought to be imminent, and residents of Long Beach, San Pedro, Palos Verdes, and Santa Monica expected the Japanese navy to show up over the horizon. The US military took control, and the entire area from Santa Monica Bay to Malibu was lined with defenses. The beaches were closed, and water activities prohibited. Japanese fishermen and farmers in the area were sent away to inland internment camps. Curfews and nightly blackouts changed life not just on the Vanderlip estate but also all along the coast. Cars navigating the Pacific Coast Highway couldn't use their headlights. Accidents were common, as were injuries and death. Living at the beach was getting dangerous, restrictive, and unpleasant. To hide any signs of night light, Ron painted the windows and Betty hung black curtains.

Horses, Walnuts, and Putting Out Fires

In 1942, Betty and Ron decided to move inland to be farther away from the threat and nearer to my father's parents and two sisters. They bought a ten-acre walnut farm on Telephone Avenue in North Chino, where they rolled up their sleeves and began a life with lots of work and little fun. Together, they started a chicken farm, tended walnut trees, and manufactured jewelry.

Although my mother later confessed that our father had not wanted any children, three years later she became pregnant again. In May 1944, one month before my mother's due date, the Navy indicted Ron over military equipment missing from a storage yard in Terminal Island, San Pedro. Apparently, my father was secretly seeing a woman who was engaged to a man who worked in the yard and knew about the equipment's disappearance. To get even, the jilted fellow reported my father to the military police. We will never know how my father got the equipment to Chino, or if he planned permanent possession. He was convicted on twenty-two counts of stealing government property: a tractor, lumber, tools, paint, and rope for his farm in Chino. He was sentenced to a military prison for three years of hard labor, but he managed to get out in one year for good behavior. Nevertheless, while he was away, my mother had to manage the walnut farm, work as a dental hygienist, take care of me, and give birth to a second child.

June 9, 1944

Medford Mail Tribune from Medford, Oregon
Page 3

Also Los Angeles, June 9 (U.R) Lt. Ronald H. Heldreich, terminal island transportation officer, convicted by a San Diego court-martial pn 22 counts of stealing government property has been sentenced to three years at hard labor, 11th naval district officers confirmed today. Heldreich was charged with stealing a tractor, lumber, tools, paint, rope, and other implements for use on his Chino, Cal., farm.

Medford Mail Tribune article of Ron in trouble
with the law June 9, 1944

My sister, Gloria, was born in June 1944, delivered by cesarean section about a month after our father was imprisoned.

Just before she gave birth, my mother took me on the train and left me with my grandparents Earl and Elizabeth, who were now living in Eureka, Utah, a small mining town south of Salt Lake City. The weeks away from my mother were long and miserable. Not only did I miss her, but also I had to adjust to my strict grandmother. I was not used to Gram's rules, and I didn't like her cooking. She made me eat everything on my plate or sent me to bed without dessert. Finally, my mother recovered and came by train to retrieve me.

Back in Chino, Mother worked as a dental hygienist and hired Mrs. Smith, a day babysitter, to care and cook for us. My sister was a year old before she met our father.

Throughout life, Betty sang words from what she called her theme song: "Accentuate the positive, eliminate the negative, and don't mess with Mr. In-Between." She endured the ordeal of my father's crimes by keeping a smile on her face, maintaining a positive attitude, and believing life would surely get better. She never talked with us about that lost year, even when we pried for details.

During this time, Betty worked for Dr. Sheffield, a dentist in the neighboring town of Pomona. After work, she occasionally socialized with friends and patients at a local bar. Among her new friends were jockeys who raced at the LA County Fairground in Pomona, as well as at other California race tracks. Betty managed to elicit betting tips on the horse races. She was a calculated-risk taker and allowed herself, armed with the jockeys' inside info, to be a small-time gambler.

Betty loved horses. One night in the bar, she bought three race-horses, sight unseen, and added them to our farm. When my father came home, he was shocked. (Her father-in-law, an accomplished horseman, had been horrified.) One of the three mares was pregnant with a foal, which Betty named Rare Sir. My parents later trained and raced Rare Sir, mostly around California. He won one or two races before they realized that owning racehorses was a full-time and costly job. With their jewelry business, chickens, and walnuts, they couldn't personally oversee Rare Sir's care and training. Yet they also realized they could not depend on trainers and needed themselves to be on the road with their horse. Soon, they sold Rare Sir and the other horses.

My parents continued to manufacture custom jewelry. People looking for original designs with quality workmanship at a fair price came to the home workshop, and business was building by word of mouth. In addition to their private customers, my parents did "ghost" work for jewelry stores in the neighboring areas of Pomona, Ontario, and Claremont. Betty picked up and delivered items, and I often drove along, eager to spend some time with her.

Ron was a skilled goldsmith and expert stone setter. Betty used her ingenuity and manual dexterity to carve wax models. The wax sculpture was part of the "lost wax" process, where a wax design is burned out of the investment material. A rubber mold is then made and used to infuse (with centripetal force) a molten precious metal, such as white gold, yellow gold, or platinum. Betty had developed her sculpting abilities while in dental hygiene school, and by now she was proficient.

Besides the sculpture, Betty mastered other processes, such as casting, repairs, and polishing. She also studied watchmaking and learned to take a watch apart, clean it, and reassemble it. She put her talent into the work and for more than twenty years working in the background, building the business but taking little credit. Some years, Betty also worked one day a week in a dental office in Los Angeles—for the good money. Ron and Betty both worked night and day, seven days a week. We did not spend much time together, other than having family dinner every night and going to the beach once in a while during summers. Family vacations did not exist. Socializing was not part of life.

In 1948, my parents sold their home in Chino and moved to Walnut, a small town in eastern LA County, where my paternal grandfather, Harry, had inherited a four-acre property with numerous outbuildings and several houses.

Betty riding Captain Banning's horse in Walnut

Harry Heldreich was an expert horseman from England who came to America in 1902. He had worked for Captain William Banning, the son of Phineas Banning, founder of the Port of Los Angeles and the early Banning stagecoach service to Southern California. In later years, the horses and stagecoaches were housed on Captain Banning's ranch in Walnut. My grandfather managed the ranch and oversaw care of the assets. After William's death in 1946, the Bannings bequeathed the ranch to Grandpa.

Mother had loved to go out there in the late 1940s to visit with Captain Banning and ride his horses. It was a preboom California setting, with rolling hills covered in eucalyptus and oak trees. Ron and Betty turned one of the ranch's wooden outbuildings into what they imagined to be the perfect jewelry studio. Life went well for a couple of years. Then one night, we were all sitting at the dinner table when a passerby ran up to the door, yelling that there was a fire in one of the buildings on the property. We ran outside and were horrified to see the jewelry shop in a mass of flames. It was too late to get anything out of the blazing building. In minutes, the shop burned to the ground. It was a total loss of jewelry and equipment.

After the heartbreak, my parents returned to Chino, built a fireproof house, and started a farm. They bought five acres of walnut trees adjacent to the acreage where we had lived before moving to Walnut. They would harvest nuts and raise chickens. They built a pink cinder-block house with a garage, and during the next year my parents poured concrete patios, put in a swimming pool, and planted shrubs. Jewelry customers came right to the house. My father worked in an interior room, and my mother's workshop was installed in one half of the two-car garage.

This was in the northern part of Chino, a drab landlocked Southern California community about thirty miles east of downtown Los Angeles and roughly the same distance from the beach. The San Bernardino mountains provided a backdrop for the landscape of orange groves, walnut orchards, and small farms. We lived a rural life. Before we were allowed to go play, we had to grade and clean huge baskets with hundreds of eggs.

It was a comfortable life in the middle of a fenced five acres, behind a locked gate. With few exceptions, only jewelry customers were allowed inside, and our father had the key. My mother loved people and preferred society to a cloistered life, but, after working with jewelry customers by day, my father did not want to welcome friends at night. Most weeknights, both my mother and father returned to work after dinner.

Ron's philandering continued, though. Women with whom he had affairs came to the house, posing as jewelry customers or "friends of the family." Each worked to befriend Gloria and me, giving us Raggedy Ann books and teacups and joining the family at the beach. Some we knew by name—Minum, Diane, Nedra. Others we didn't. It was the early 1950s, and divorce was not a viable option for Betty. She didn't want to curtail our lifestyle or separate us from our father. Her optimistic side must have led her to think he would stop his adulterous behavior so they could make a good life. But making a good life with a womanizer is not much fun for any woman—let alone a smart, freethinking, and independent one.

During the summer, when Chino weather heated up, we would drive an hour to the beach at Corona del Mar to cool off. One year we leased a trailer in Newport Beach, next to the Girl Scout Camp, where we spent the days with our mother. We swam in the bay, rowed a little boat around Lido Isle, and walked over to the Newport Beach Pier on Twenty-First Street. There, we checked out the Dory Fishing Fleet and the seedy bars. Our father came to the beach when he could get away. But soon the nightly fog kicked up my mother's asthma, so we had to give up on the trailer.

CHAPTER 5

HAWAII CALLS (1951–53)

In 1951, Betty received a letter from the Territory of Hawaii. Her older sister, Jane, and Jane's husband, Smithy, were coming to visit. Because they lived 2,500 miles away in Hawaii, and because transportation to and from the islands was scarce and expensive, this was the first time we girls would meet either one of them.

Jane had taken a ship to Hawaii in the 1930s. She took a job working for the Territory at Kalaupapa, Molokai, Hawaii's leper colony, where she met Arnold Smith, known affectionately as Smithy. They married there in 1939. Smithy was the superintendent, and Jane worked in administration at the hospital.

Kalaupapa, located on the rugged east side of Molokai, is a six-acre peninsula surrounded on three sides by a night-blue, treacherous, deep ocean. Inland, it is bounded by the world's highest oceanside cliffs. In 1866, King Kamehameha V designated Kalaupapa as a place to quarantine people stricken with leprosy, or Hansen's disease, a malady thought both highly contagious and incurable. Without choice, men, women, and children with the disease were sent to the isolated outcropping. Patients were taken by ship and dropped off near shore, where they had to swim to a life of exile. In 1873, the priest Father Damien went to Kalaupapa to comfort the lepers. He lived there until he contracted leprosy himself and died in 1889.

Jane and Smithy had no children and immediately took a liking to me. Smithy, originally from rural Virginia, was impressed that I was in the local 4-H Club and raised pigs. We talked about farming. Smithy said, "Victoria, next year, when you are twelve, you will come to Molokai." He promised to pay for my visit, meet me in Honolulu, show me the highlights of the islands, and take me back to Kalaupapa for the rest of the summer.

"Oh, please let me go," I begged my parents. After some days of conversation, my mother and father relented. I was elated to think I would be the first one to follow Aunt Jane to Hawaii.

After nine long months of school—and daydreaming about palm trees and pineapples—summer finally arrived. I was twelve, old enough to be allowed as a visitor to the leper colony. Jane and Smithy asked me to arrive on a certain date, which meant leaving school two weeks early—no tragedy for me. The teachers gave me a couple of Hawaii-related assignments and cleared me to go. I packed new summer clothes and a bathing suit. On the drive to the Los Angeles airport, I was beset by contradictory feelings. Thoughts of leaving my family for almost two months and traveling 2,500 miles by myself scared me, but the greater part of me wanted to take this adventure.

I was a minor, so Pan American Airways required that my mother board the four-engine plane and hand me off to the stewardess, who presented me with a Pan Am wings pin and a duffel bag. She assured my mother she would take good care of me as they both escorted me to my seat. After a hug and a kiss, I sat down and fastened my seat belt. "So long," my mother said by way of parting. (She didn't believe in saying "goodbye," thinking it was too final.) "You are going to have a summer adventure, and I will be thinking of you. If you like it, maybe I'll go and see it for myself next summer."

After a ten-hour flight, the plane landed in Honolulu. Escorted by the stewardess, I was the first passenger off the plane. Aunt Jane and Uncle Smithy, accompanied by their group of friends, greeted me with a royal Hawaiian welcome. We exchanged hugs and kisses galore, and each person bequeathed me a sweet-smelling flower lei of plumeria, carnation, or tuberose.

We were houseguests of the Fords, friends of Aunt Jane and Uncle Smithy. Bill Ford was the manager of Dairyman's Dairy where he and his wife, Mike, lived in a Hawaiian plantation–style house situated where the Waialae golf course is now—in Kahala, on the back side of Diamond Head. Its five-acre lawn stretched to the ocean; its lush gardens were filled with tropical plants and trees, including coconut, mango, papaya, and plumeria.

Mike, wanting me to have a good time with friends my own age, invited some neighborhood kids, Sheila Fletcher and the Hoagg brothers, to the house for parties. Bill barbecued, and Mike set up a badminton court on the front lawn.

After ten days, Aunt Jane and Uncle Smithy took me on an extravagant sightseeing trip. We flew to the Big Island of Hawaii, where we stayed at the Volcano House, Hawaii's oldest hotel. Built in 1846, with massive timbers in a hunting-lodge style, it perched on the northeast rim of the Kilauea caldera, affording a view down into the volcano. I had never seen such a huge hole in the ground—an impressive sight for a farm-town twelve-year-old.

Uncle George Lycurgus, a Greek American who was also the Volcano House's owner and manager, was a fixture, known for his cribbage games. By now, Uncle Smithy had taught me to play, and I lasted three rounds with Uncle George. We played in the main hall, near a twenty-foot-high lava-rock fireplace with glowing flames. The walls were lined with Hawaiian landscape paintings and photos of Uncle George with famous visitors to the hotel.

After a few days at Volcano House, we drove to Hilo and stayed at the old Naniloa Hotel, overlooking Hilo Bay. From there we drove north, through the sprawling Parker Ranch to Waimea town. I had never seen so many cows or expansive, grass-covered hills. Then we were on to the rambling, two-story Kona Inn, built in 1928 and designed to blend in with the palm-lined seashore. There was a Hawaiian pili grass shack on the grounds, a replica of where Hawaiians lived in ancient days. We explored the City of Refuge and then flew on to Maui, where we stayed in one of the few hotels on the island. The funky, two-story wood structure was located in Wailuku, a sugar plantation town, and I experienced Maui as the agricultural island it was in the 1950s. We took Andrew Airline, a single-engine plane, first to the town of Kaunakakai, Molokai, and then down along the cliffs to Kalaupapa for the rest of the summer.

In Kalaupapa, Aunt Jane and Uncle Smithy dreamed up hedges against boredom. I spent many hours with Lulu, the chubby, good-natured Hawaiian maid, who taught me hapa-haole hulas like "Hukilau" and "My Little Grass Shack in Kealakekua, Hawaii." Uncle Smithy often picked me up and drove me around the peninsula as he made his work rounds. On weekends, Father Patrick and other priests came over to drink, play cards, and indulge me in a game of cribbage. During the week, I played cards with Sister Carmelita and several other nuns.

One magical day, we hiked into the next valley, Waikolu. After making our way along the rocky shoreline, we walked inland along the streambed, picking watercress and *Coix lacryma-jobi*, the gray beads used for necklaces and known locally as Job's tears. Aunt Jane and Uncle Smithy took me to a rocky beach where I picked and cautiously ate my first raw 'opihi, a limpet the size of a quarter, a Hawaiian delicacy. It was rubbery and crunchy and tasted like seawater.

One morning, Uncle Smithy took me to the pier where the Young Brothers barges landed twice a year with food supplies—it doubled as a popular fishing spot for patients. This was my first time fishing. A local man offered to bait the hook for me, and I noticed he had only stubs for fingers. Many patients contracted leprosy in the era before antibiotics, and I soon became familiar with mutilated and scarred noses, ears, fingers, and toes. I never grew used to the sight.

I fell in love with Hawaii. When I returned to Chino after the summer, I was miserable. I lay in bed and moped. This was not my normal behavior. After days of questioning what I liked about Hawaii, my mother decided she had better go see what had made such an impression on me. Years later, the character Gordon Gekko in the movie *Wall Street* proclaimed, "Moping, for lack of a better word, is good. Moping works." It strikes me that in that moment, my moping, and the reaction it elicited in my mother, changed our lives forever.

The following June, my mother and Gloria followed in my footsteps. Aunt Jane, Uncle Smithy, Mike and Bill Ford, and other friends greeted them royally. Aunt Jane and Uncle Smithy always dressed elegantly, and that day Aunt Jane wore a belted dress, nylon stockings, and heels. Uncle Smithy was decked out in a white shirt, a tie, a dark brown business suit, and large, dark glasses.

Uncle Smithy, Betty, and Gloria arrival to Hawai'i, summer of 1954

They began their stay, as I had, with Mike and Bill Ford. The Fords' house was perfect for company, made for entertaining, with sprawling hiki'e and pune'e (double- and single-size beds turned into couches) to accommodate guests after the four bedrooms filled. The huge kitchen held industrial refrigerators, countertops galore, and an eight-burner gas stove with two large ovens. Bill loved chopping vegetables and cooking for large groups. (I particularly loved his chicken hekka, a gingery stir-fry with vegetables.) The Fords were enthusiastic and gracious hosts; everyone was welcome. They had a tight-knit social group that consisted of eight or ten couples who gathered on weekends.

A pet mynah, Jake, was often the center of attention with his non-stop jibber-jabber, entertaining anyone and everyone who would listen.

A sign on the wall over his cage read PEOPLE ARE NO DAMN GOOD. His main mantra was "shit tabaggo." The alcohol flowed freely, and there were oodles of jokes and much storytelling.

Starved for this kind of interaction, my mother loved the Hawaiian lifestyle—it made for a bracing hurricane after the still air of Chino. The Fords were becoming lifelong friends, Hawaii a lifelong love.

After several weeks as a houseguest of the Fords, my mother heard about some of their friends, Dr. Willers and his family, who needed a house-and-dog sitter while they went on vacation. Their house was located on the water, four miles toward Koko Head, on Kalaniana'ole Highway. It was roomy and a comfortable place to spend the better part of a summer, and my mother had use of the car.

Soon she sent for me. I had been staying in Atherton, in Northern California, with her sister Cay and her family. Aunt Cay had a luxurious house with a miniature golf course and a swimming pool, surrounded by trees, but I didn't like my uncle. I pined for Hawaii. I almost ran onto the Pan American flight out of San Francisco. Once I arrived in Hawaii, Mother extended our vacation through the end of the summer. We had six weeks together, and with each passing day, she and Gloria and I fell more and more in love with island life. As if the tropical flora and fauna, the balmy air, and the beaches weren't enough, there was something else: a new sport.

Discovering Waikiki

The beach in front of the Willers' had a shallow reef that prevented easy swimming. So every day we drove the family car to Waikiki Beach, picking up our new friends along the way, including Sheila Fletcher, the Hoagg brothers, David Hicks, and whoever else from the neighborhood wanted to join us. We parked ourselves in front of the original Outrigger Canoe Club, located at the time between the Royal Hawaiian Hotel and the Moana Surfrider. (Now it sits farther south, by Diamond Head.)

A friend of the Fords had heard my mother talk about wanting to learn to surf. He advised her to look up the famous and fun-loving Charlie Amalu. The next day, my mother did just that. Situated at stations in front of the hotels along Waikiki Beach, the beach boys were proficient watermen whose occupation—and preoccupation—was to share the secrets of the sea with visiting malihini, or newcomers. They taught surfing and took tourists out in six-man canoes to catch waves. The beach boys were also raconteurs, entertaining tourists with ho'omalimali, which literally means "flattery." They were charismatic, and they knew how to charm women.

CHAPTER 6

THE GOLD COAST (1954–55)

When we arrived home from our summer vacation, Betty began to work on Ron. My father himself visited Oahu several weeks later. He could not fathom our infatuation. In fact, he telephoned my mother every day, complaining about anything and everything. During most of the year, delicate breezes flow from Honolulu's cool valleys to the ocean. My father was unlucky—he visited during a hot and muggy October with Kona winds that blew onshore. But my mother's mind was made up. We were moving, come hell, high water, or Kona winds.

Gloria and I counted the days until we could go back. My mother had vowed to return the day after Christmas 1954. The jewelry business thrived in December, and she knew my father needed her. She also knew that after the holiday orders were filled, there would be more money for the move.

During the next months, every Saturday afternoon, my mother, my sister, and I gathered in our kitchen and listened to *Hawaii Calls*, hosted by Webley Edwards. This radio show was broadcast live from the historic Moana Hotel, facing the break known as Canoes. We listened to the surf murmuring in the background behind the melodic cadences of Hawaiian music and the voices of singers like Alfred Apaka, John Kameaaloha Almeida, Nina Kealiʻiwahamana, and even Hilo Hattie.

47

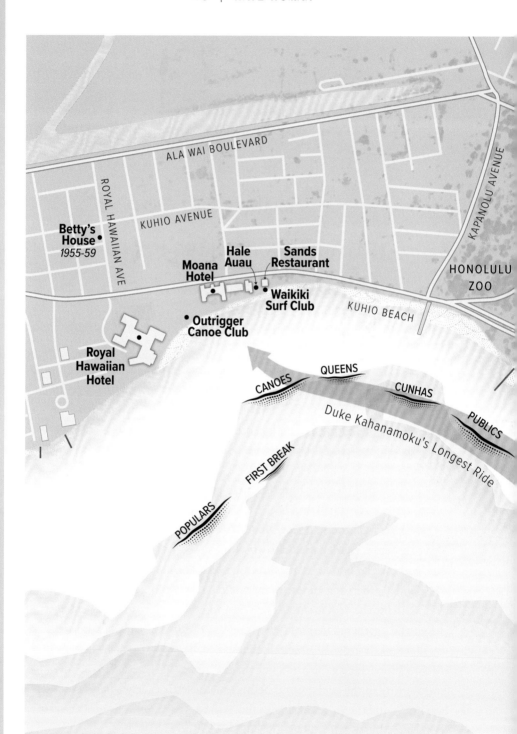

ALA WAI BOULEVARD

ROYAL HAWAIIAN AVE

KUHIO AVENUE

KAPANOLU AVENUE

Betty's
House
1955-59

Hale
Auau

Sands
Restaurant

Moana
Hotel

Waikiki
Surf Club

HONOLULU
ZOO

KUHIO BEACH

Outrigger
Canoe Club

Royal
Hawaiian
Hotel

QUEENS

CANOES

CUNHAS

PUBLICS

Duke Kahanamoku's Longest Ride

FIRST BREAK

POPULARS

DIAMOND
HEAD

MONSARRAT AVE

PAKI AVENUE

KAPIʻOLANI
PARK

KALAKAUA AVENUE

DIAMOND HEAD ROAD

**War Memorial
Natatorium**

**Castle
House**

**Dad Center
Apartments**
1954-55

CASTLE'S

TONGG'S

Waikiki, 1960

1 km   0.5 km   0

0.5 miles   0.25   0

December 26, 1954, the day we would return to Hawaii, finally arrived. Our suitcases were packed, and my father was driving us to the Los Angeles airport. Off we went on a United Airlines flight. My mother and father had decided that my father would stay behind to sell the house, pack up the furniture, and ship the tons of jewelry manufacturing equipment to Hawaii so they could start a new jewelry business.

Thanks to the ministrations of Aunt Jane and Uncle Smithy, we rented the guest cottage at an eight-story complex called the Dad Center Apartments. Our one-bedroom wooden cottage sat on the street side, at the front. We had a little kitchen; my mother slept in the living room, and Gloria and I shared the bedroom. It was a small but ideal place for us, as it was located on the Gold Coast of Waikiki. We lived at the base of Diamond Head, with the ocean on one side and spacious Kapiʻolani Park on the other. Our backyard was the park's three hundred acres of lawn, edged with white, yellow, and pink blossoming shower trees. The World War I–era Waikiki Natatorium War Memorial swimming pool was a few minutes' walk away—it was an impressive saltwater pool set right into the ocean and had served as the site of swim meets and Olympic trials.

Best of all, the Tonggs surf spot was right in our front yard.

We moved into the cottage the day after our landlord's sixty-eighth birthday and were immediately taken in by Lily and Dad Center, who were friends of my aunt and uncle. It was kismet that we three befriended Dad Center at a time when we were sorely in need of a father figure.

George David "Dad" Center, the son of a Scottish sugar plantation manager, was born on Maui in 1886 during the reign of King Kalākaua. He had moved to the island of Oahu and spent a few years in Waiʻanae, where his father was the sugar plantation manager, before moving to Waikiki. The family lived in a two-story, five-bedroom oceanside house at the Diamond Head edge of Waikiki Beach. Dad's father died in 1897, when he was eleven, and he eventually inherited the house and property where Dad spent the rest of his life. Dad had known Waikiki when royalty enjoyed surfing and canoeing and when the area was mostly a scattering of shacks on a palm tree–lined and taro-planted wetland—a marsh believed to be a haven for mosquitoes. In 1921, dredging began to drain the swamp and build the Ala Wai canal. During the 1920s and

'30s, sand was imported from Manhattan Beach, California, via ship and barge, and used to widen Waikiki Beach.

Dad was a towering but quiet man with brown hair, twinkly blue eyes, an impressive nose, and, always wore a battered straw hat and sneakers. He was a swimmer, surfer, outrigger canoe paddler, canoe sailor, body surfer, fisherman, oarsman, yachtsman, volleyball player, golfer, basketball player, soccer player, track-and-field man, and football player—an athletic wonder. As a young man, he inspired thousands of boys and girls to partake in athletics. In 1920, Dad Center was a coach for the American Olympic swim team, and he was later recruited to coach swimming at Punahou, Honolulu's most prestigious private school. It was his legions of protégés who affectionately dubbed him Dad. He was captain of the outriggers for the Outrigger Canoe Club from 1910 to 1932 and received many awards for paddling and racing Hawaiian canoes in the 1930s. This earned him another moniker, the Father of Canoe Racing, and the *Honolulu Advertiser* called him "one of the island's most famous personalities." In short, the man was a legend.

Dad and Lily had built the apartment complex in 1954 on the family property. They were more than just our landlords; they included us in their social celebrations, and we visited with Dad just about every day. He regaled us with water stories that included the royals King Kalākāua and Prince Kuhio; his youth, first on Maui and later at Wai'anae; his early days living in Waikiki; and his experiences coaching ten swimmers from Hawaii, including Duke Kahanamoku, for the 1920 Belgium Olympics.

One day, we were discussing swimming styles and Dad said, "Girls, go put on your bathing suits, and let's walk over to the natatorium." When we arrived at the 140-meter pool, he said, "Get in the water and show me how you swim the crawl." My mother swam a width of the pool and passed her test. Dad said, "Vicky, now you." He watched me swim a lap and motioned me over to the side of the pool, where he was standing. "That was pretty good," he said, "but it could be so much better if you bring your arms more directly in front of your face. He then gave me some pointers so that I could pull the water with more force. "Your kick is okay, but make it faster by using more strength."

Then, of course, there were his stories about surfing—just what interested us. His most memorable waves included the more-than-a-mile "long ride" that Duke Kahanamoku made famous. "Kahanamoku's epic ride started near the base of Diamond Head at a mystical south-shore break called Kalehuawehe, now known as Castles. (The modern name honors James Castle, who lived in a three-story yellow home on the shore.) The spot is located on a second-reef site about a half mile outside the natatorium and breaks only when a massive south swell produces waves that are ten to twenty-five feet high. (Otherwise, no waves form there.) It is the beginning of a rare mile-long series of left slide breaks that curve into the center of Waikiki, finally diminishing in the sand in front of the Moana Hotel. In 1917, Duke made the ride on what he said was the biggest wave he had ever seen. Legend has it that Duke's was the longest ride in Waikiki history. The ride was simulated interactively at an exhibit on Duke Kahanamoku at the Bishop Museum in 2015. Dad recalled that his own "longest ride" happened in 1917, the same year Duke's was reported. Dad's ride was less celebrated but just as dramatic, at least the way he told it. To say my mother and I were inspired is an understatement.

Showing his natural inclination to mentor other athletes—not to mention his willingness to trust his protégés—Dad loaned my mother his redwood surfboard. She referred to the board as the *Queen Mary* of surfboards, describing it as a "fourteen-foot, solid redwood plank floater." She said she could sit outside all the other surfers and catch most of the waves before anyone else could. But there was no skeg for mobility and turning. Once she started on a wave, the board and Betty cleared a path, wiping out everyone who got in their way. It may have been a free board, but it was heavy and dangerous—she had little or no control.

Betty wanted her own, more modern board and soon heard about a master craftsman named Joe Quigg. Before Joe had moved to Hawaii from Southern California, he had been known for making the best lightweight boards for women. His early lightweight shortboard was called the Darry-lyn, followed by a series called Girl Boards. Having one of Joe's surfboards meant that women could no longer be pushed off waves and dominated by men. Betty ordered a ten-foot Joe Quigg balsa board for around $85. As soon as she picked it up, she surfed every day in the clear, warm water of Waikiki. She was bitten by the "surf bug," as she called it. She even said she was "spastic" about the sport. And she started to make surfing friends.

Betty with Joe Quigg surfboard in Waikiki

Where were you born wave
To come to rest on the beach
Reborn as backwash

—Betty, 2009

In January, when school started, and thanks to Uncle Smithy's advice, I was enrolled at Punahou, the private school founded by missionaries in 1848. Congregationalists from New England who started arriving in Hawaii in 1820 wanted their children to attend school in the islands, rather than going by ship to the United States. The first private school west of the Rocky Mountains, Punahou has produced many accomplished alumni, from former US president Barack Obama to former AOL CEO Steve Case to NFL star Mosi Tatupu and Pipeline master Gerry Lopez, along with legions of doctors, lawyers, merchants, and prominent executives. Tuition was $350 per year; my father thought the private school was too expensive and too elitist, and he argued that we should attend public school. But my mother put her foot down and enrolled me as an eighth grader. There was not yet an opening for my sister, so she had to wait two years to enter as a seventh grader.

In Chino, we had attended a public school with a large Mexican immigrant population. Expectations were low, and I was not the best student. Punahou was a college prep school with high standards and burnished traditions. As a result, the school insisted I repeat the eighth grade. This was a comedown, but after a few semesters of serious study, I was able to bring my grades up to passing. Socially, it was not so straightforward. Most of my classmates had been together since kindergarten. There were many cliques, and I did not fit in well. Complicating matters, I was a year older and my classmates seemed immature. Somehow, I managed to make friends with some of the Hawaiian boys on the football team, which only made me even less popular with the girls. It was a lonely place for the first few years.

Surfing became my escape. Every day after school, I headed home as quickly as possible, headed straight to the beach locker where I stored my surfboard, and hit the waves. Soon I met new friends, as well as some schoolmates who also surfed at Waikiki. The surfing friendships partly made up for the lack of camaraderie at school (although eventually, some of my Punahou classmates became lifelong friends).

Betty did not surf all the time, of course. She had brought along a few tools and began carving out of wax small Hawaiian mythological characters known as menehune. In Hawaiian mythology, the menehune are described as dwarves or "little people." They are said to have inhabited the islands centuries before the Polynesians arrived from the South Pacific. Hawaiian lore claims they lived hidden in deep forests and valleys, far from the eyes of humans, and came out only at night. Betty, fascinated with this folklore, created a series of menehune charms: a pearl diver, a poi pounder, a ukulele player, a conch-shell blower, and male and female canoe paddlers. She also carved a surfer on a hot-curl wave. These miniature wax figures were later cast in gold and sold as pendants, earrings, and charms for bracelets. (They were Betty's creations, but my father took credit on the government patent.)

In six months, my father sold our Chino house to a doctor for cash, shipped the crated jewelry-making equipment, and joined us. But he was never thrilled about living in Hawaii; it took him away from his fiefdom—a Chino he loved dearly. Not only do I believe he regretted the move, I don't think he ever forgave us for starting this family adventure. In fact, I think my father consciously or subconsciously tried to punish me, the instigator. There were already strains in our relationship. Even as a young girl, I was depressed after a conversation with him because he always dwelled on global financial problems that neither one of us could fix. My father had a bleak outlook and usually focused on the things that were wrong. I was temperamentally more like my mother, and as she and I forged ahead with surfing, I grew further and further away from my father, and he from me.

After Ron joined us in June 1955, we rented a house in Kahala for a few months, but Kahala was not for us. By the end of the summer, we moved to a three-bedroom, two-story white house at 352 Royal Hawaiian Avenue. The house was located half a mile from Queens Surf Beach and the Canoes surf break in the simple, quiet Waikiki of that time.

The district was lively and often full of sailors when a navy ship came to port, but nothing like the overly crowded commercial hub it is today. It was a lowkey, uniquely glamorous spot in the 1950s, before passenger jets and statehood. There were no high-rises; shops and small houses lined the streets, along with a sprinkling of two-story apartment buildings and very few hotels higher than six stories.

Ron and Betty in Waikiki at Lao Ye Chai Restaurant

The *Lurline* and *Matsonia* passenger liners arrived and departed once a week. Local men and boys dove for coins thrown from the ships at the Aloha Tower, a lighthouse built in 1926 in Honolulu Harbor. Pan American Airways flights took ten hours from California, and the number of tourists between 1957 and early 1959 averaged only 180,000 a year. (Today, approximately ten million visitors bring in close to $15 billion in revenue each year, and Waikiki is a madhouse.)

In the 1950s, Hawaii was expensive and out of reach for the average, middle-class person. Instead, it was a destination for an elite crowd from around the world: dignitaries, movie stars, professional athletes, and industrialists who had the time and money to soak up the pleasures of paradise.

Our life in Waikiki was never dull; we brushed shoulders with young and old visitors from all over the world, as well as movie stars, heads of state, and sailors from the Peruvian and French navies. It was a cosmopolitan life, despite the fact that we were on a small island 2,500 miles from anywhere.

Gloria and I shared a roomy bedroom upstairs on the street side of the house. We had a covered balcony for observing the sights below—especially an eccentric woman across the street who had been a madam during World War II. We watched her come and go, dressed in large, flower-printed muumuus and gaudy makeup, her orangey-blond hair swept high on her head.

My parents once again started a jewelry business, this time in the downstairs bedroom. Located in the center of Waikiki, the house worked out perfectly for a business. Betty surfed every morning, and after a full day of work, she had little time for cleaning, shopping, or laundry. To keep the house in order, she gave me a generous allowance of $20 per week and put me in charge of the housekeeping. At fifteen, I liked this responsibility for several reasons. First, I was able to get a driver's license and take the yellow Cadillac convertible to do errands. Best of all, I liked having the money to buy clothes at Liberty House and ice cream treats at the local drugstore.

The Surfing Life

In 1955, my parents joined the Waikiki Surf Club. It was an unpretentious club located at the Diamond Head end of Waikiki, in front of the Waikiki Tavern, and very different from the exclusive Outrigger Canoe Club, located near the Royal Hawaiian Hotel. At the Outrigger, members had to be voted in. By contrast, the Waikiki Surf Club welcomed all. The enrollment fee and annual dues were modest. The club promoted surfing and water sports and gave locals affordable access to canoes and surfboards.

John Lind started the club in 1948, in the basement of the Waikiki Tavern. He became president and launched the Waikiki Surf Club with six hundred members he recruited in the first few months. The club also initiated several ocean events that stimulated public interest and fostered competition: the Diamond Head Surfboard Paddling Championship, the Molokai Hoe outrigger canoe race, and the International Surfing Championships at Makaha—the first big-wave surfing event.

ON THE BEACH AT WAIKIKI

When we joined the Waikiki Surf Club, it was a ramshackle wooden building in front of the Waikiki Tavern—a hole in the wall open air wooden structure on the beach, with a sand floor—and a funky place, but happy and fun. A few Adirondack chairs offered seating. On a three-tiered set of wave-watching benches, dirty-footed, half-clothed members were often stretched out sleeping. Most of the club members were local Hawaiians.

The club was a great place to hang out in between waves, and it offered not just a perfect view of all the surf spots in Waikiki, but access to them, too. To enter, we made a circuitous walk toward the water from Kalākaua Avenue, passing rows of surfboard lockers, Earl Akana's Hale Auau (which rented surfboards), and the Merry-Go-Round Bar. Reaching the sand, we meandered along the front opening of the perfectly named Waikiki Sands—an early, open-air, all-you-can-eat restaurant. We skirted the edges, gazing at plates of food on tables just inches from the pathway.

One of the finest six-man canoes in Waikiki, the *Malia*, made on Hawaii Island of blond koa wood and sold to the Waikiki Surf Club by Dad Center, was beached in front of the clubhouse when not out on the waves. Surfers and paddlers relaxed there after surfing or canoe paddling, engaging in benign banter that we would describe as "talk story." But, their being surfers, the island yarns would often veer into exaggeration, or what we called hoʻomalimali. (To older Hawaiians, the word meant "flattery" or "cajoling," but to us younger surfers it indicated that the tales were only marginally believable.) Some of the members would bring their ukuleles and jam, or kani ka pila. The singer and composer Kui Lee, known for his melancholy ballads and his untimely death, even played at the club.

Ron was willing to give surfing a brief try—he even bought a Joe Quigg surfboard—but he wasn't taken with the sport. He preferred to work at home and take an occasional swim or walk. There were, we later learned, other diversions.

For her part, every morning at dawn before starting her workday, Betty, wearing only her bathing suit and a shirt, rode her bike down to Waikiki Surf Club, where she kept her surfboard. She usually surfed at Queens and Canoes, which were right in front of the club. More and more, she loved the thrill of traveling across a wall of breaking water, standing on a surfboard just in front of the wave's curl. Leg bang-ups, rib bruises, and hematomas did not deter her lust for this sport. In fact, she often got scraped up—in most pictures, she is wearing a bandage. But surfing was her proving ground, her inspiration, and her salvation.

Betty surfing with John Lind and Beach Boy Mud Warner, 1956

Betty on a wave in Waikiki

Ethel Kukea and Betty in front of Waikiki Surf Club

Betty was mastering the Waikiki surf and beginning to feel the sport's ineluctable pull. She set some of her impressions to paper:

Surfers are a breed of people,
A restless group of people who go searching the world for a
hot curl.
They are besieged with a disease that is incurable—one more
wave is never a cure,
It is only the challenge of man against the elements/surf.
The bigger the wave, the greater the challenge.
Victory leads one on in search of bigger waves
and defeat only means more practice at surfing.

Betty also started to follow the ocean surfboard paddling races, which were held every year between Christmas and New Year's in front of the Moana Hotel. The competitors raced out around a marker off Diamond Head and back to Waikiki. These races drew large crowds, including tourists whose numbers swelled because of the Christmas season. Paddling built arm muscles and strength for surfing, which made it attractive to Betty. She also loved the idea of racing other women.

The champion female paddler, Ethel Kukea, was a five-foot-ten-inch athlete with blue eyes, a light brown bob, and a strong, square jaw. Born in Long Beach, California, Ethel was a year younger than Betty. As a girl, Ethel was introduced to surfing by her older brother Lorrin "Whitey" Harrison, who made his first surfboard at age eleven. In 1931, he made boards for an early surfboard manufacturing company, Pacific Ready-Cut Homes. (The balsa surfboards were called Swastika Boards and sold for $25.) In 1941, when she was twenty-seven, Ethel traveled by ship with Loren to Hawaii from her home in Santa Ana. Soon, she married a Hawaiian fireman, Joe Kukea, and had three children. Ethel was a graceful surfer, a champion paddler, and a fierce competitor. Her main interest, beyond being a mother and wife, was to live a simple beach life, with its focus on ocean activities.

From childhood, Betty was driven to achieve her personal best. She loved showing her muscles. Both she and Ethel were energetic, and ocean sports came to be a proving ground and a means to physical and emotional well-being. They were high achievers motivated by the status and recognition that came from a win. Betty may have been more worldly than Ethel, but the two women socialized and were more than just cordial to each other, both on land and out in the surf. They were close friends, but Betty's secret goal was to beat Ethel.

Betty had Joe Quigg make her a board specifically for paddleboard racing. It was twelve feet long, narrower and lighter than a board made for surfing. Finally, the day after Christmas in 1955, Betty faced Ethel in the Waikiki paddle race, leaving the Moana Hotel and heading to the buoy off Diamond Head and back. Ethel was in front on the way out to the buoy, but after they rounded it and heading back to shore, Betty slowly pulled ahead. They stayed within yards of each other ahead for the rest of the race to shore. They were neck-and-neck all the way to the finish line, but Betty prevailed.

Although Betty cared about her appearance, she was a modest, no-frills dresser and didn't like to spend money on clothes or shoes. She mostly went barefoot or wore slippers and kept her hair in a short bob, almost a pixie cut, for surfing. Bikinis were alive and popular in Tahiti, but in the 1950s, Hawaii women were still wearing boxer-type shorts with a bra-like top. Betty preferred a white Linn's two-piece bathing suit, which became her trademark. These 100 percent cotton duck suits were durably constructed, with a substantial top and shorts, and they wore like iron. Inspired by sailor suit pants, the shorts had two sets of four buttons running vertically up the front to a waistband. The Linn's suits were perfect for surfing. Everything stayed in place if you were tossed and thrashed by a wave. Always practical, Betty also realized she could bleach her suit over and over and wear it for years.

Betty's favorite month to surf was July at Waikiki, on the first-break waves. Being out in the water at dawn, watching the sunrise, looking up to Mānoa Valley as rainbows formed and faded from one side to the other, was, to her, the perfect way to start a day.

Hidden energy
Surfing the big waves is like
Dancing with nature

—Betty, 2010

Betty started to meet and get to know fellow surfing regulars. In addition to Ethel and her husband, Joe, they included Lord Blears, Rabbit Kekai, Conrad Cunha, Blue and Violet Makua, Jane Kaopuiki, Scooter Boy, Wally Froiseth, and Anne and George Lamont. Betty also befriended Clarence Maki, the first Waikiki photographer to strap a camera to his board and get pictures from a surfer's perspective. Then there was Dad Center's friend Duke Kahanamoku, the five-time Olympic medalist, Hollywood actor, Honolulu sheriff, and surfing icon.

A more humble surfing pal was the Chinese Hawaiian police detective Jimmy Wong. Between wave sets, Betty and Jimmy had some time and got acquainted. He urged her to take a trip out to the west side of Oahu, to Makaha. Jimmy told Betty she had to check out the beach, the waves, and his new "kit" house.

Betty surfing with Jimmy Wong and Wally Froiseth, 1956

CHAPTER 7

WESTSIDE STORY (1956)

In 1956, my mother decided to take Jimmy Wong up on his offer. Our family, plus Gloria's Honolulu friend Mele Kukea (Ethel and Joe's daughter and friend), drove west thirty-six miles from Honolulu out along the leeward side of Oahu to visit Jimmy and his wife, Emily. The drive took us past the plantation towns of Aiea, Waipahu, and 'Ewa. At that time, sugarcane fields stretched from one town to the next. After a rightward bend in the two-lane Farrington Highway, just past 'Ewa and the Campbell estate, all of a sudden there stretched before us a series of round hills, or volcanic tuff cones, that jutted out into the cobalt sea. We continued along the rugged seashore, past the sleepy towns of Nanakuli, Maili, and Wai'anae. Gray-green mountains rose to the right, punctuated by spacious, mile-wide valleys. We passed bountiful farms, wooden shacks, and Quonset huts, all surrounded by gardens with swaying coconut palms and plumeria trees flowering in pinks, yellows, and whites. We witnessed country living at its best; pigs, chickens, horses, and dogs lived largely unpenned in yards and fields.

After an hour's drive, we arrived at Makaha Beach. The Hawaiian word "makaha" means "fierce, savage, ferocious." Legend has it that a group of Hawaiian bandits once lived in the area, robbing travelers and generally

65

pillaging. This storied area lies at the foot of a great green valley carved like an amphitheater into the backside of the spectacular and most sacred spot on the coast, Mount Ka'ala. At 4,040 feet, the mountain is at the head of the Mākaha and Wai'anae valleys, the highest peak on Oahu, and celebrated in many a traditional song. Its craggy volcanic summit sits starkly against an impressive backdrop, an azure sky with phantomlike clouds.

Makaha was originally home to native Hawaiians who farmed, fished, and later traded with schooner ships anchoring in the bay. The Mākaha stream gave life to the lush valley, which is also home to the Kane'aki Heiau, a lava-rock temple. The heiau, which the Bishop Museum restored in the 1960s, is said to be the best-preserved temple on Oahu. Built in the 1600s, it is dedicated to Lono, the god of agriculture and fertility. A large stone there, Pohaku o Kāne (Stone of Kāne) is named in honor of another major god, regarded still as the guardian of the heiau. Kamehameha the Great is said to have worshipped here, and the site was in use as a war heiau until his death in 1819.

After overzealous traders wiped out the native sandalwood crop, Mākaha Valley became home to sugar and coffee plantations. In 1898, a single-gauge railroad was put in to link the Wai'anae Coast with Honolulu and also to transport sugar in the other direction, around Ka'ena Point, to the processing mill in Kahuku. In 1946, the sugar plantations of Makaha and Wai'anae closed because of a lack of water. In 1947, the Mākaha ahupua'a (a pie-shaped area of land running from the top of the mountain to the ocean) sold for $1,250,000 to Chin Ho, whom *Time* magazine called Hawaii's Chinese Rockefeller. Chin Ho sold off the prime beachfront property in order to develop projects in the valley.

But Makaha was still mostly untouched in 1956. Mākaha Valley leveled out at the Pacific coastline, and just below a craggy mountain softened by grasses lay a half-mile crescent of clean-swept, white-sand beach—the most beautiful strip Betty had ever laid eyes on. The water was clear and clean, with multiple hues of turquoise and teal. Fish abounded. The water temperature averaged seventy-four degrees. The air was dry and sunny in the daytime and balmy at night.

We found the Wongs' address on Farrington Highway and turned into the driveway. The Wongs were quite a couple. Jimmy, in addition to being a police detective and regular surfer, was a musician and singer. Emily was an accomplished hula dancer and a hostess at the Willows Restaurant in Honolulu, famous for its sprawling grounds, koi fishponds, shrimp curry, and coconut pie. Their three children included James Kaʻupena Wong, soon to become one of Hawaii's premier chanters.

After a brief welcome greeting, Jimmy and Emily gave us a tour of their Lindal Cedar house, proudly showing off each little bedroom. Keeping with Hawaiian-style hospitality, they invited us to have something to eat. Jimmy motioned us over to their dining room table while Emily surprised us by pulling out a coconut pie from her refrigerator. We devoured it over our afternoon conversation.

After we finished eating, Jimmy stood up from the table, smiled, and said, "Come, Betty." The diminutive police detective walked out the door, onto his front lawn. My mother followed, and we followed her. Jimmy walked to the beach and a few steps along the sand, to an overgrown weed-and-sunflower-covered beach lot, one with the same ocean view as Jimmy and Emily's. He pointed to a small FOR SALE sign posted on the ocean side of the property.

Betty pulling out for sale sign after first seeing Makaha property. From left to right: Anne Lamont, Gloria, George Lamont, Mele Kukea, and Betty

Gloria came running up from the beach, where she was playing with Mele Kukea. Both of the curious girls followed us up the gradual bank of sand. My mother walked up to the sign on the property and stood for a moment, looking around. Since her childhood trip to Santa Monica, she had dreamed of living near the ocean. She turned around and looked at Mount Ka'ala and the steep surrounding mountains. Then she took another look at the white-sand beach in front and the surfable waves breaking off Kepuhi Point. Betty paused for a moment and then leaned over and yanked the For Sale sign out of the ground. She shook the loose, sandy dirt off the stake, held the sign over her head, and said, "This has to be mine."

She remembered the advice Dad Center's realtor wife, Lily, had given her in response to the abundance of land for lease in Honolulu: "If you ever come across a piece of fee-simple property on the beach, if at all possible, buy it."

Back in Waikiki, first thing Monday morning, Betty and Ron contacted Mr. Fitzjohn, the property owner, and met with him to make a deposit. Betty and Ron paid $13,000 for the thirteen-thousand-square-foot lot. (Later, Betty was able to buy some additional footage on the street side, increasing the lot size to sixteen thousand square feet.)

Betty could barely wait to get back to Makaha and surf the waves. She called Ethel Kukea and Clarence Maki to tell them about Makaha— the surf she had discovered and the property she had just bought. They decided to drive out on the following weekend. During the 1950s, there were no hotels or places to rent for the night, so everyone planned to camp on the beach.

Saturday morning, my father said he had work to do and would stay home. Making jewelry was my father's joy and a bit of an obsession. Besides swimming, his main recreation was smoking cigars and reading Kipling. Gloria, too, was a bookworm, but she enjoyed the beach. By this time she was a twelve-year-old, more chubby than athletic. I was a tall, gangly sixteen-year-old and somewhat hesitant about leaving Waikiki surf for the unknown, but game. My mother, now forty-three, was in prime physical shape. We packed up our beach clothes; loaded our surfboards, some food, and minimal camping equipment into the Caddy; and set off for a Makaha that would soon be ours.

When we arrived at the public beach, no one else was out on the sand or in the water and not a single car was parked. We had the place to ourselves. We parked on the side of the road so we could easily unload supplies. Our friends pulled their cars in next to ours. Anne and George Lamont arrived first. Ethel and Joe Kukea brought their three children, and Clarence Maki brought his wife, Edna, and their son.

We measured the waves by the face, in comparison with the height and stance of a person riding the wave. The waves were around four feet high and perfect for the adult surfers. Gloria and I lay on the beach and enjoyed the sun, taking an occasional swim to cool off. The younger Kukea kids swam and played in the shore break, splashing and catching little waves.

In the late afternoon, we all gathered driftwood scattered along the beach, and Betty made a fire. She was the designated cook for the teriyaki beefsteaks. Everybody had brought something to contribute: snacks, rice, salad, vegetables, and cookies. We had a feast on the sand.

After dinner, we stoked the bonfire and made s'mores, talking and listening to the sounds of the ocean in the background. The warmth of the fire on our bodies balanced the coolness of the night air. After a day in the sun and water, we tired early. Mother, Gloria, and I curled up in our blankets next to one another near the fire while the rest of the group adjourned to their makeshift tents. As we fell asleep, we watched a spectacular light show of shooting stars.

The first signs of dawn and the sound of breaking waves woke us up. Betty stoked the fire and began preparations for breakfast. Later, she cooked bacon and eggs that we ate with bear claws from the Alexander Young Bakery. After breakfast, we cleaned up and got ready for another day.

"Vicky," my mother said, fixing her greenish-blue eyes on mine, "we need to go surfing."

Big Waves

In the beginning, Makaha seemed like a terrifying place to surf. It was a right slide, where the wave breaks from left to right, and suited our stance. Mother and I were both regular-footed surfers: We faced the wave, rather than keeping our backs to it, as a goofy-footed surfer would do (right foot forward and left foot back). We were now in new, treacherous territory, though, as the waves were thicker, stronger, larger, more powerful, and more challenging than those at Waikiki. At first, their force and size frightened me. On that first morning, I spent a lot of time paddling back and forth between the farthest outer edge of the lineup and the channel. Sitting too far away from a place to catch a wave, I paddled endlessly for mounds of water that were impossible to catch. Sitting in the channel, looking sideways at the curling waves, was intimidating, for they looked much bigger than a straight-on view. I was petrified but trying to overcome my fear. My mother kept motioning me to where she was sitting, saying, "Come over here, where you can catch a wave." Finally, after much prodding, I got up enough courage to paddle over into the lineup, where the waves formed near an underwater coral head. Finally I caught my first wave. That was it for me—I was over the hurdle.

During the next three years, my mother, Gloria, and I went out to Makaha as much as possible, camping on our beach lot as soon as escrow closed. Besides the weeds on the property, there was a leftover World War II military refrigerator box that measured about ten by sixteen feet. We called it our icehouse and stored our stuff there: a barbecue, cooking equipment, dishes, towels, surfboards, and anything we needed for camping. If it rained or if there were too many mosquitoes buzzing around, we slept in the icehouse.

Kehau Kea came out occasionally and surfed with us. Five foot eight, with shoulder-length brown hair and brown eyes, she was a classmate from school, a surfing and paddling friend from Waikiki, and one of only a few native Hawaiian female surfers. She had surfed at Waikiki for only three years but was strong from paddling canoes. She had a lively sense of humor, and we liked surfing with her. (In 1958, she was queen of the sixth annual Makaha International Surfing Contest.)

Other women surfers of the time included Keala Stibbard, Anona Naone, Del Wong, Jane Kaopuiki, Joan Kalahiki, Mozelle Angel, Christie Daniels, and Marge Philips, although most women were not regulars at Makaha—they came out only for contests. But there was a growing group of male surfers who would come to Makaha and sleep in their vans or in cars with the backseat removed to make a bed. No one wanted to miss the glassy early-morning surf conditions. Several were young, bright, newly hired teachers just out of college from school who became friends. Peter Cole came out alone in his woody. A Stanford graduate and math teacher, Peter was, at six foot two, an athletic big-wave surfer. He was friendly, wise, and gracious. Fred Van Dyke was shorter yet muscular, with a quirky personality and a fascination with health and fitness. He taught science and was an early environmentalist; years later, when he commuted to work by car from Sunset Beach, he wore a gas mask. Fred was just starting to date his future wife, Dee, an art teacher. After surfing, we often made a bonfire on the beach, drank beer, and had a lot of laughs.

My mother and I concentrated on learning to surf Makaha. Gloria was happy to sit on the beach or swim. My father was less enchanted with the place and made the trip only occasionally. We three were fine without him and his grumbling. This was also my mother's time away, a chance to do her own thing. She was coming to love the sport more than she loved her life with him.

Our first surfboards were made of balsa wood, stretched ten feet long, and weighed about forty pounds. But as we improved our surfing skills, and as changes in materials made surfboards lighter, faster, stronger, and more maneuverable, we wanted better options. We upgraded to models from Hobie Alter, Pat Curren, and Renny Yater. The cost of these surfboards was steadily escalating, but we were usually able to sell an old one for enough money to justify buying a new one. Not that we were frivolous about casting off old boards, especially if we liked them. If the balsa-wood beauties got dinged from the rocks or gashed by other boards, Betty fixed them. She would sand the ding, put new fiberglass over the hole, and cover the patch using epoxy and resin. She did this as proficiently as she carved figurines.

This was a time before leashes, so wiping out on a wave meant the board usually washed a quarter of a mile (or more) to the shore. Often, local children would grab the boards before we caught up with them and catch little waves in the shore break. In 1957, one of those kids was Rell Sunn, then seven years old. Betty befriended the girl, who clearly had a feeling for surfing. Years later, Rell said that before she could read books, she could read the ocean, the tides, and the wind.

This was also a time before buoys and broadcast predictions about swell size and surf conditions. The only way to know about the waves was to drive out to "the country" or telephone Dok and Marie Klausmeyer, the first people on Makaha Beach with a telephone. (A surf spot in front of their house is named in their honor.)

Most waves defied the simple statistics on a surf report. Each had a personality and a character of its own. We thrived on the challenge of figuring out how the textures and depth of the ocean bottom would affect the swells. We had to learn the language of waves, and where to sit by lining up a house on the point with a coconut tree onshore. Besides the long right slides, Makaha had a tricky backwash. The backwash formed a short-lived but rideable counter-directional wave produced by a wave's whitewater hitting the shore and retreating into the next incoming wave. My mother and I learned to ride these waves together.

> To describe a wave analytically, to translate its every movement into words, one would have to invent a new vocabulary and perhaps also a new grammar and a new syntax, or else employ a system of notation like a musical score or algebraic formulas with derivatives and integers.
>
> —Italo Calvino

Soon my mother and I were surfing regularly with a new group and beginning to feel part of something larger than we were. New friends—Peter Cole, Fred Van Dyke, George Downing, and Johnny McMahon—gave us tips. All the men were generous with their knowledge. We sought their advice, and our abilities improved.

In 1956, we were part of the beginning of surfing's resurgence. Although it is referred to as the sport of kings, surfing was for everyone in ancient Hawaii—kings, commoners, women, and children. Disputes were settled and bets were placed on surfing competitions. Hawaiians put aside work during a four-month period between October and January known as the Makahiki, when celebrations included lots of surfing, in addition to music, hula, and large feasts. But such festivities waned as Westerners arrived, and especially after 1820, when New England missionaries began exerting their influence on Hawaiian culture. By 1850, surfing had become a rare sight around the islands.

One hundred years later, fewer than two thousand surfers were reported on the island of Oahu—some of them native Hawaiians, some of them kama'aina (residents whose families had been in Hawaii several generations), and some of them newcomers like us. Surfing spots were not crowded; there were plenty of waves for all to catch, and it was a friendly sport.

California Comes to Hawaii

In 1953, news of a twenty-foot winter wave at Makaha was published in newspapers in California and throughout the world, stoking interest in surfing. An iconic Associated Press photo showed Buzzy Trent, Woody Brown, and George Downing streaking across a mountain of water. By 1954, early surfers from California started flowing in—Walt and Flippy Hoffman among the first. A larger group followed in 1956 and rented the Sumidas' Quonset hut, next door to us.

These California surfers were an entertaining group, and there was always a lot of surf talk. The most mesmerizing and melodramatic tales came from Buzzy Trent. Buzzy was a twenty-nine-year-old native Californian, raised in Santa Monica, who had come to Hawaii in 1953 to surf Makaha. He had a muscular build, a larger-than-usual head, a wide face, blue eyes, and light-brown hair. An all-state football player and natural athlete, he was considered a pioneering big-wave surfer. He was also an extroverted motormouth, reporting his surf quests in semi-stuttering verbiage. One tale was of the "gigantic" Cloudbreak outside Maili Point;

another concerned the big shark that made a home near the surf spot. In all his tales, Buzzy was the protagonist fighting not-always-benign nature. Sometimes he would spew out his dream: to conquer forty-foot behemoths at Ka'ena Point, the barren promontory beyond Makaha and Makua, where Hawaiians believed souls left the earth for the hereafter.

As an ambitious young woman surfer, even if I could never match his rhetoric or his bravado, I soaked up Buzzy's surf stories. We became friends, and he coached me on safety practices for larger waves. Buzzy demonstrated the best way to handle my board when paddling through an incoming breaking wave, shared surfing techniques for larger waves, and tipped me off on how to locate the best position in the lineup. It surprised me when, in 1963, *Surf Guide* quoted Buzzy as saying, "Girls are intended to be feminine, and big-wave riding is definitely masculine. Women should not surf the bigger waves (more than six feet), as they are more emotional than men and have a greater tendency to panic, and panic can be extremely dangerous in big waves." However, Buzzy was often misquoted. Ironically, one afternoon in 1958 with ten-to-twelve-foot surf at Makaha, Buzzy, Peter Cole, and I got caught inside a set of breaking waves, and it was Buzzy who panicked and yelled for me to let my board go. Thinking he knew best, I followed his advice. After diving under a couple of waves, it became difficult to keep my head above the white water. Luckily, Peter saw me in trouble and paddled over, I got on his board, and, lying prone, we rode the white water to shore. Perhaps by 1963, Buzzy had forgotten that both men and women can panic in big surf...

Most of the young California surfers had a great sense of humor. They were pranksters, joking constantly with their surf buddies and any other audience. They loved to brag about their best rides and their biggest waves, and they spun comical yarns about other surfers. Life was performance with many of them; they competed to see who could pull off the craziest and wildest capers. Here we were, my mother and I—a couple of women surrounded by spirited men. We were like sponges for their chatter.

The surfers from La Jolla, California, spun stories about politically incorrect escapades at Windansea Beach. As they told it, in the early 1950s, someone's father had brought home some full Nazi uniforms with guns. A few of the guys dressed up in the uniforms, slung the guns over their shoulders, and went to the top of the beach cliff. They climbed into a six-foot-wide drainage pipe and slid down the hill and out onto the beach, where they acted like German Gestapo men tormenting tourists. Wayne Land and Pat Curren inhaled lighter flames and blew rings of smoke out of their mouths. Tiny Brain Thomas was an easy target for teasing, as he did many mindless things, like going to a surf spot and leaving his board behind.

Tom Carlin, from Coronado, California, was a small but strong, towheaded, retired Navy SEAL who had been on the US Navy's Underwater Demolition Team. He was an amazing waterman but took the cake with his unconventional antics and miserly habits. He knew how to live on pennies. While attending San Diego State College, he lived in a tent in the nearby canyon, using the cafeteria for meals and the gym for showers. When he came to surf in the winter of 1956, he built a tree house on Sunset Beach, located in Dr. Brandt's backyard. The doctor lived in Honolulu and probably never realized that Tom and other surfers were living in his trees. The following year, when Tom visited with his girlfriend, Wendy, a dark-haired aspiring actress, they camped out on Wayne and Judy Lands' front yard at Kepuhi Point (which, at the time, we called Makaha Point). Tom dove for fish and lobster to augment the food he stashed and guarded intently in the Lands' refrigerator. He even went so far as to mark the frost line on the Kool-Aid container with his finger to make sure no one was filching. Occasionally, he would present a lobster to Betty, probably because she knew how to cook it perfectly. His ingenuity and love for the simple life amused us.

The Makaha Break

Waikiki offered visitors and islanders alike a variety of waves, and the tourist mecca was dotted with breaks popular for their summer swell: Castles, Publics, Cunhas, Queens, Canoes, and Populars. But it was the big winter-swell surf of Makaha that enticed those of us who were up for a more bracing experience. From October to March, the waves at Makaha were at their best. They could be mild in the morning and turn into twenty-five-to-thirty-foot behemoths by afternoon.

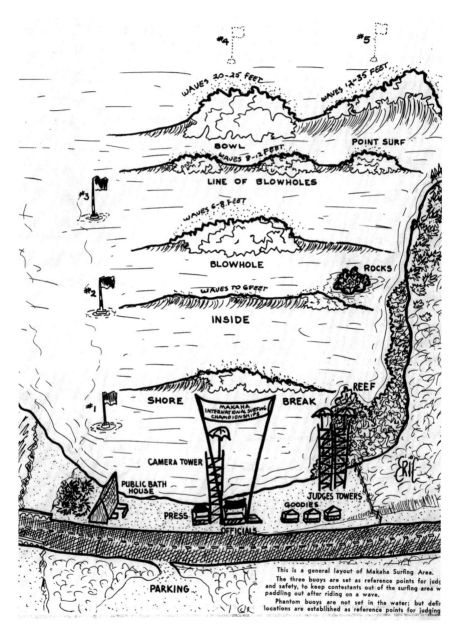

Petersen's *Surfing Magazine*'s guide to Makaha Breaks in Hawai'i, 1966.
Courtesy of the Preston Peterson Archives

Generally, Makaha has four main breaks. Three are right slides, and one starts out as a left but continues halfway in as a right. Each break depends on the size of the swell and varies slightly. At Kepuhi Point, on the Kaʻena Point side of the bay, eighteen-to-twenty-foot-high waves break; in the bowl, farther inside, the swell starts as a left and midway in the bowl turns into a right with fifteen-to-twenty-foot waves; there's a midsection with ten-to-twenty-foot waves, and farther in is the blowhole with six-to-ten-foot waves—the hole in the coral bottom provides a lift and steepness that make it easier to catch the wave. Finally, there's the inside break, with smaller waves. We were never quite up to the point or the bowl-size surf. It was just too big for us.

My mother and I surfed Waikiki and Makaha together for about seven years. Surfing was not just a sport; it was our lifestyle, something that brought us together during a precious time in our lives. Surfing dominated our thoughts and conversations: When could we get away to go surfing; where should we surf; and, afterward, how had each ride played out? Some of the people who shared our obsession became lifelong friends. We were all enthralled with the physical thrill, the chance to flirt with danger, and the self-satisfaction that grew from mastery. Surfing gave us strength, physical stamina, and mental toughness as we continually challenged ourselves. The ocean's beauty and the feeling of being one with nature gave us a sense of well-being. Just as important, it released us from our quotidian lives.

Despite our enthusiasm, we were spooked by the unsettling stories of the monster waves on the North Shore at Waimea Bay in 1943, when Dickie Cross lost his life and when Woody Brown barely survived being washed up onshore with his swim trunks ripped off. Both Betty and I aspired to bigger, better waves, though not quite as big as what we witnessed Buzzy Trent, Peter Cole, George Downing, and others ride. The contemporary big-wave surfer Andrea Moller describes the feeling at the start of riding a big wave: "It's almost a moment of silence because it's just you and this huge volume of water and this pat-pat-pat of your board on the surface." Moller rides much larger waves than we ever dared, but she puts into words what we experienced. Once you make the drop and turn up into the wave's wall, she adds, "you're in this silent glass world of water, and you're in so much risk, and yet you're so driven that it almost feels like there's a pause."

One early spring morning in 1959, shortly before I was to graduate from high school, my mother and I got up at dawn and went out to the lawn to check the surf. We could see from where we stood that there was a good six-to-eight-foot swell running, with glassy waves. Both of us were born tall—she was five feet, eight inches; I was five ten. An eight-foot wave would tower above us. We couldn't resist. We waxed our boards with extra fervor—on waves like these, we couldn't afford to slip—then hoisted them up under our arms and headed out the front lawn and down the beach. We walked a quarter mile along the bay, side by side, our bare feet crunching on the cool morning sand. I recalled how, during my childhood, I had longed to spend time with my mother, but she was always busy working. I had plenty of diversions (a horse, a swimming pool, and ten acres of space), but there was always something missing—Mother. Finally, in my late adolescence, I found that time with her through surfing. Now I was walking into adulthood and a life of many unknowns. There was a comfort in walking with her that morning, of sharing the anticipation of the surf—which contained its own unknowns.

To minimize paddling, we walked past the sandy channel to the edge of the reef. Back on our right, a golden disk was just coming up over the mountain, and a delicate breeze was flowing down the valley. The air was filled with the pungent, musty smell of kukui nuts that had washed onshore. We paddled out, dodging a set of incoming waves, to a spot we knew well, the break area. It was just past the underwater coral heads, and our preferred place to wait for a wave. Fred Van Dyke and Johnny McMahon, the manager of an upscale Waikiki men's store, were already sitting there, waiting. We arrived at our spot and sat upright, our bare legs straddling the boards and plunging into the cool morning sea. We both thought there was no better way to start a day than being immersed in clean, blue-green salt water, looking up to the emerald Mākaha Valley in the distance, and feeling the ocean's liberating and healing powers. It was exhilarating and peaceful at the same time. We exchanged "howzits" and chatted about the beautiful surf conditions, my mother's building project, and Fred's eighth-grade science class. Then we waited, looking out to sea, watching for new mounds of water forming on the horizon—the first sign of a set of incoming waves.

A set approached. Adrenaline flowed. My mother and I stayed put, letting Fred and Johnny take the first wave—after all, they'd gotten there first. We claimed the next one for ourselves. We jockeyed for position with a few little paddles and the foot motion needed to turn our boards toward shore. As the wave approached, we each lay flat, readying ourselves. I paddled like mad to catch the wave and felt my board rise in the water. My mother did the same. In a few seconds, the power of the wave replaced our paddling and propelled our boards. Putting both hands on our boards, we both popped up to a standing position and angled to the right, heading down a wall of water that was starting to crest and feather with ocean spray. It almost felt like flying. I was gliding down the face, keeping as close as possible to, yet just ahead of, the breaking wave as it crested with white water. My mother was doing the same, standing on my right side, closer to the outer edge. Several times throughout the ride we both slowed down, stalling before turning and cutting back toward the breaking wave, shooting down the wall of water closer to the curl for added acceleration. The ride went like that, both of us slowing down, cutting back, speeding up, always in tandem. It was one long, unforgettable moment. Not one of symbiosis, exactly, because we had parity as we rode that wave. It was more simpatico, or deep sympathy—a kind of knowing each other and each other's styles and moves. It was an experience of elemental connecting with the waves, with the ocean, and with each other.

In six months, my view toward surfing would change. I lived through a heart-wrenching and harrowing day of surfing in Hale'iwa. In a few more months, my mother and I would leave Makaha to travel internationally as a mother–daughter surfing duo. A few more months after that, I would leave Makaha again, for life in San Jose, California, as an awkward young bride. My life and my mother's would soon start to flow in their own directions, sometimes diverging, sometimes converging, sometimes just running in parallel. But that morning, as we sped across the wave together, I couldn't help thinking how lucky we were.

CHAPTER 8

WAVE RIDING GOES COMPETITIVE

(1957–59)

My mother used to tell me, "Vicky, surfing is going to be big." She encouraged me to keep notes. "You should keep the notes; I'm busy living this sport," I would answer. We were aware of the beginnings of the surf media when we lived in Waikiki and the artists John Severson and Bruce Brown were selling their surf-art from the curb of Kalaukaua Avenue. Such artists helped plant the image of surfers as nonconformists and free spirits. Later, around 1958, Severson and Brown started to produce surf movies, starting with *Slippery When Wet* and culminating in Brown's best-known film, *The Endless Summer*, in 1966. In the meantime, Severson founded *Surfer* magazine in 1962. By the 1970s, surf culture was in full force and had spread nationwide. Fast-forward to 2016: Twenty-three million people around the world defined themselves as surfers. Though she thought she was prescient, Betty would be blown away by these statistics.

Much of the initial frenzy might be traced to the annual Makaha International Surfing Championships. The inaugural contest, in 1954, was advertised as the first big-wave competition in the world. It invited

Hawaii contestants to test their skills against counterparts who had developed in different waters. As it grew each year, the contest attracted thousands of sightseers, and the name Makaha became synonymous with the most challenging big-wave spot in Hawaii. Waimea Bay was only just starting to get attention, and it would be decades before spots like Northern California's Mavericks, Maui's Jaws, and Portugal's Nazaré became familiar to surfers.

The first year of the Makaha competition, in the fall of 1954, there was no surf, so paddleboard races became the main attraction. That year and the following year were for men only. The third year, word was getting out and women were welcomed for the first time. Incredibly, 110 contestants signed up. Between eight thousand and ten thousand spectators flocked to Makaha on January 15 and 22. The major events included senior men's surfboard riding, women's surfboard riding, junior men's surfboard riding, mixed tandem, senior surfboard paddle, junior surfboard paddle, women's surfboard paddle, mixed tandem surfboard paddle, and a four-man run-swim-paddle relay. Betty entered the women's surfing division, along with Ethel Kukea, Violet Makua, Joan Kalahiki, Esther Kalama, Mary Ann Hawkins, Christy Donaldson, and Cynthia Hemmings. Her competitive spirit kicked in, and she had some good rides, and took second place behind the winner, Ethel Kukea, her congenial friend and competitive foe. Betty won the paddling race, where Ethel took second.

Carlos Dogny, the president of the elite Club Waikiki in Lima, Peru, was one of the judges at the 1956 surf meet. The son of a French army colonel and a Peruvian sugarcane heiress, he was a handsome, sophisticated playboy who traveled between homes in France and Lima. He had learned to surf under the tutelage of Duke Kahanamoku during a 1938 visit to Waikiki. Carlos had returned to Peru with a hollow surfboard that the Duke had given him. There, he encouraged his friends to surf with him at Miraflores, a site just a few miles outside Lima that had a break with long, easy, rolling waves similar to those at Waikiki. In 1942, Carlos founded a Club Waikiki in Miraflores to have a gathering place for his surfing cronies.

Left: Vicky, Carlos Dogny and Betty in front of Outrigger Canoe Club, 1956

Betty Goes to Lima

During the third Makaha International Surfing Championship, Dogny was particularly impressed with the women he saw surfing the arduous waves. In South America, the sport was considered strictly for men. Back in Lima, Carlos convinced his fellow Club Waikiki members that they should bring surfing women to Miraflores to stir interest among the women of Peru. Carlos (on behalf of Club Waikiki)

invited them, along with other contest winners from the Waikiki Surf Club, to visit Lima. A Hawaiian surfing team was formed in March 1956, consisting of the male champion of the Makaha meet, Conrad Cunha, and the runner-up, Rabbit Kekai, as well as my mother, Ethel and Joe Kukea, Anne and George Lamont, and Roy Ichinose.

The team would be in Lima for a month as guests of Club Waikiki. It was an invitation of a lifetime, but each team member had to pay his or her own airfare. Betty was determined to go and financed her own trip. Articles in the local newspapers created hoopla about the trip and solicited donations. The Waikiki Surf Club put on benefits and luaus to raise funds for the surfers who couldn't swing airfare. That was the main expense—once the team arrived in Lima, the Peruvians would pay for lodging and lunches at Club Waikiki.

Each team member was required to get a health certificate and a police background check. Neil Blaisdell, the mayor of Honolulu; Dan Liu, the chief of police; and Allen Bostick, the vice president of the Waikiki Surf Club, all wrote letters of introduction. Duke Kahanamoku, the ambassador of Hawaiian surfing, supported the trip and posed with the team for public relations pictures in front of the Outrigger Canoe Club. This was the first time Betty met Duke, although she had surfed alongside him at Waikiki.

Gloria was in grade school that spring, and I was a sophomore in high school, so we stayed home with our father. My mother said she hated to leave me, her surf buddy, behind, but she thought I was too young to make the trip. She consoled me by saying that if I could win the next Makaha championship, she was sure we would get invited back to Lima

Waikiki Surf Club
P. O. BOX 2299
HONOLULU, T. H.

February 23, 1957

Club Waikiki
Lima, Peru.

Gentlemen;

This letter will introduce Mrs. Betty Heldreich, a member in good standing of the Waikiki Surf Club, Honolulu, T.H.

Mrs. Heldreich is attending and competing in the Surfing competitions at Lima, Peru as Second Place winner in the Women Senior surfing competitions as judged by the International Surfing Championships Association at Makaha, Oahu, T.H. for the year 1957.

Yours very truly,

Allen J. Bostick
Vice President
Waikiki Surf Club

Betty's introduction letter for Lima surf competition, 1957

T. Umeda

Five Set For Peru Surfing Meet

Two men and three women surfers will compete in the International Surfing Meet at Lima, Peru, starting March 8.

They are Conrad Canha, Rabbit Kekai, Ethel Kukea, Betty Heldreich, and Anne Lamont.

Funds are being raised for Mrs. Kukea, Canha, and Kekai. The others will pay their way to and from the championships.

To raise funds a benefit surfing movie will be shown at the Long House in Hawaiian Village Friday at 7:30 p.m. and a professional wrestling show will be sponsored at the Auditorium Sunday evening. Fifty per cent of the wrestling tickets sold by the fund raising committee will be contributed to the fund. Reservations for either event may be made by phoning 999094 or 729421.

The Advertiser is also accepting contributions to the fund.

George Lamont will accompany the surfers to Peru.

In the photo are, left to right, Duke Kahanamoku, who wished the surfers good luck, Rabbit Kekai, Conrad Canha, Ethel Kukea, Betty Heldreich, and Anne Lamont.

The *Honolulu Advertiser*'s article on the surfers set for Peru, February 13, 1957

Betty leaving Honolulu for Lima, Peru

as a mother–daughter surf duo. (My mother was practiced at putting such challenges before me. At five years old, I had to swim across the neighborhood pool to be given a bike.)

Throughout the trip to Lima, each member wore a yellow, short-sleeved, button-up shirt with red Waikiki Surf Team lettering that was the team uniform. Each also took a balsa surfboard. The combination of club style and trusty equipment drew attention to the ad-hoc team.

The surfers flew on Pan American Airways from Honolulu to San Francisco, then south, touching down in Los Angeles on the way to Panama for an overnight stop. Betty clowned around with five-foot, six-inch Rabbit Kekai in the hotel swimming pool, practicing acrobatics for the tandem display. It was decided then and there that Betty, at five foot eight, was too large for a tandem event. The team boarded a Panagra plane to Lima, landing in the wee hours of the morning. In spite of the inconvenient arrival time, a gregarious welcoming committee greeted the team at the airport with lei and South American hospitality.

The surfing team stayed at the Gran Hotel Bolivar, a luxurious inn off the Plaza San Martín, in the center of downtown Lima. Every morning, the group hailed a rickety taxi called a *collectivo* to take them to the club. Lima, congested with old American cars, had chaotic and boisterous traffic. Horn honking was prohibited, but Betty never forgot the unhappy drivers who yelled out swear words and banged their arms on the sides of their cars as the *collectivo* made its way through the city traffic. It took twenty minutes for the *collectivo* to reach the residential area of Miraflores, with its tranquil, tree-lined streets and gated two-story houses.

Club Waikiki sat on the edge of some barren cliffs just above the Pacific Ocean. It was a split-level, bamboo-sided structure with men's and women's locker rooms, a pool, squash court, kitchen, and dining room. This was beach elegance at

Hotel where the team stayed in Lima, Peru

its best, a far cry from the Waikiki Surf Club in Hawaii. Its membership was filled with the Lima elite. Spanish-speaking Quechua men welcomed visitors onto the upper level, where trophies and pictures of founding members covered the walls of the lobby. The Quechua men were about four feet tall, menehune size, dressed elegantly in white dinner jackets, long black pants, and white gloves.

The Hawaiian team surfed, socialized, and ate delicious lunches on the veranda overlooking the sea. The islanders always found themselves surrounded by eager questioners who wanted to know about surfing and canoe paddling in the Hawaiian Islands, where both were year-round activities. (Surfing was only a summer sport in Lima, as the winters were cold and gloomy, with little sun.)

Club Waikiki was a special gathering place not just for surfing but also for playing squash, working out, and taking long lunches with pisco sours. Afterward, members went home for a siesta before returning to work around four. Most men worked until eight at night and dined between ten and eleven. Elegant late-night parties were held at the Club Waikiki, as well as at country clubs, restaurants, and nightclubs in Lima. The team listened to bands playing cha-cha, merengue, and tango music and danced into the early morning.

Club Waikiki coat of arms

There was no sand in front of the club, only small pebbles that rolled around with the incoming and outgoing tides. This made it tough to get to the water, so narrow planks of wood were set out for walking to the sea. It was against Waikiki Surf Club policy to carry your own board; beach boys carried surfers' boards from the lockers to the shoreline and waited to carry the boards back when surfers returned.

Gentle waves rolled in, and the only people surfing were club members. The Miraflores break was different from Waikiki, where the wind generally blows offshore, meaning that it blows across the land, toward the sea, causing the waves to break more slowly and cleanly. It also keeps waves from breaking until they become steeper and more powerful. At Miraflores, sometimes the wind blew onshore, making the waves sloppy and the water murky. (Onshore winds increase waves' tendency to topple

Betty at Club Waikiki watching the surf competition

over earlier and make for a less exciting ride.) But offshore, onshore, it didn't matter to Betty—she was happy to be there.

There were plenty of other adventures. Besides surfing at the club, the team also surfed at a break known as Kon Tiki at Punta Hermosa, an hour's drive south of Miraflores. One afternoon, Ethel, Rabbit, and Betty were paddling out to the breaking sets. A wall of warm water formed into a wave ahead, and they saw that it was full of dangling jellyfish. "Let's get out of here!" Rabbit yelled, then led the trio on what may have been their fastest-ever paddle to shore.

The main event of the trip, the surfing contest, was held during the second week of March at Kon Tiki, because it boasted a bigger break than at Miraflores. The break started a half mile out, with large, defined lines of swells coming in off the point. (In this regard, it was similar to the Makaha break.) The contestants were judged on the size of the wave, their position in relation to the part of the wave that broke, and the length of the ride. As usual, Betty's chief competition was Ethel. Even though Ethel had been surfing for twenty years, Betty had been practicing at Makaha. She was ready. The waves were rolling in from the point and perfect for the women's event. The competitors entered the water, made the long paddle out to where the waves were breaking, and vied fiercely. Betty caught bigger waves with longer rides and earned the top score. She finally beat Ethel at surfing. She was awarded a two-foot-high silver cup (For twenty years, the trophy sat on a bookshelf in the living room.)

Years later, when Betty reminisced about her surfing days, she would say, "I think Ethel was the better surfer. I was just lucky. I was in the right spot for the biggest waves of our heat, and I was able to catch them."

Betty with 1st place women's surfing trophy

The Peruvian style of aloha impressed Betty. The magnanimous hosts took the team into their homes and shared their families, as well as their beaches. She bonded with Alfredo Granda, Carlos and Rosalba Rey, Richard Fernandini, Augusto and Pancho Wise, and Carlos Edwardo Arena, among others. They fell in love with Betty, and many visited her in Hawaii over the next forty years. Betty made a special connection with Cesar Barrios—a suave, brown-eyed banker of Spanish descent. They stayed in touch, and he came to see her in Makaha in 1962. For Betty, competing and partying in Peru was all part of her surfing adventure, not just a long way from Hawaii, but even farther away from Chino or Salt Lake City. She was beginning to see that surfing was providing her much more than just a new challenge. She felt appreciated and loved for who she truly was—perhaps for the first time in her life.

The Waikiki Surf Club members welcomed the Hawaii/Lima team home with a special ceremony. Friends and key members gathered at the club to present Betty with lei and congratulate her on her performance. The *Honolulu Advertiser* ran an article that included a photo of Betty holding her trophy, along with the caption "Champion Surfer Returns from Peru."

Life on Royal Hawaiian Avenue was never the same again. Betty became more and more disenchanted with being married to a workaholic womanizer. Her new Peruvian friends were happy-go-lucky and fun-loving, but they were also sophisticated Latin men who could afford to enjoy every minute of life—and to share that enjoyment with her. Not so for Ronald Heldreich. He and his social life were limited to customers and lady friends; otherwise, he preferred a hermitic existence. Betty had tasted how pleasurable life could be and, by contrast, how humdrum their marriage had become.

The 1957 Makaha International Surf Contest

By now, my mother and I were at Makaha every weekend there was surf. We put the top down on the Caddy and wedged our surfboards vertically behind the front seats. The boards were ten feet long and stuck far up into the air, but no one seemed to mind. We would joyfully head for the

Westside, which is how we (and most surfers) referred to the entire coast on the west side of the Wai'anae range.

This all worked perfectly well, but I had started to form my own identity and wanted my own surf mobile. After a lot of cajoling, my mother let me buy a green Austin station wagon for $125 from a class-mate, singer Robin Luke. It seemed like a good price, but practically every-thing started breaking down. We had to rebuild the car, first purchasing new tires and then a water pump. However, my mother took care of the repairs and even joined me on surf expeditions to the North Shore.

In 1957, during my junior year, my mother and I both entered the Makaha International Surfing Championships. Finally, it was my turn to compete. I beat not only my mother but also Ethel Kukea, winning the women's division. The *Honolulu Advertiser* wrote, "The Makaha surf contest obliged with a spectacular show yesterday, with waves ranging between 6 and 20 feet. As expected the duel between Ethel Kukea, defending champion, and chief challenger, Vicki Heldreich, who said she surprised herself, stole the show. Blond Miss Heldreich continued where she left off last week, when she topped eleven other qualifiers, by staging a spectac-ular performance to outscore Mrs. Kukea." Ethel was not pleased to be outdone by a seventeen-year-old malihini who had been surfing for only four years—not to mention that I took the title away from her.

Even my schoolmates and friends were impressed. Although my first name was misspelled in the article, I was thrilled to win and happy that people were taking note. Given what was happening on the home front, the positive attention was a boost for my self-esteem.

Surfing was beginning to bring me attention. An early magazine article about surfing, "They Ride the Wild Waves," appeared in the June 14, 1958, *Saturday Evening Post*. The article featured my surfing friend and Punahou classmate Kehau Kea, as well as my mother, Rabbit Kekai, George Downing, and me. I was happy to receive the kind of notice my mother had been enjoying.

CHAPTER 9

NEW HORIZONS (1959–60)

In January 1959, I was eighteen years old and a senior in high school. I came home one day and went straight into the kitchen to get a snack. My mother was usually working in her shop at this time, but she stood calmly near the sink, waiting for me, wearing plaid Bermuda shorts and a sleeveless white blouse. She asked briefly about my day at school. After I told her it had gone okay, she walked toward the back door, motioning for me to follow. My father was working in his shop, a couple of rooms away. I could tell she wanted a private conversation.

Once we were out of his hearing range, my mother launched right in: "I have something to ask you, Vicky. After twenty-two years, I don't want to be married to your father anymore. I want a divorce, but I want to make sure it's okay with you. How would you feel about it?"

Even though I was young, I had been a firsthand witness to my father's capers with other women. Also, he had been slowly alienating me with his unrelenting verbal one-upmanship. Although part of him tried to be a good father, sometimes Ron Heldreich was outright unpleasant. I especially resented his unwelcoming attitude when my friends came to visit. My junior year, I had invited a favorite boyfriend, Ray, to dinner. My father refused to come downstairs to join us.

The worst, though, was my sense that he fooled around with anyone and everyone who would have him. Over the past few years, my father's behavior had become more and more outrageous. When he did come out to Makaha, he often snuck around with the wannabe surfer Anne Lamont. Once I became a teenager, it was hard for me to come to grips with the meaning of his behavior. I wondered how my mother could put up with it and realized how excruciatingly painful his infidelity must have been for her. I had begun to wonder if I myself could ever trust a man. So I told my mother that I didn't like the way my father had been acting and that I believed she would be much happier without him. I was fine, I said, totally fine, with her decision.

"I hope Gloria will feel the same way," she said, reverting to her sometimes formal style of speech, slowing down her sentences and dispensing with contractions. "She is young. I am worried about how she will take it. But if you think you will be okay with this, I am going to move ahead and ask for a divorce right away." My mother stood firm and, without emotion, held my gaze. "We will have to move out of this house. Finishing the school year might be hard for you girls. I want him to be good to you and Gloria, so, as far as a settlement goes, I am going to go easy on him. I will only ask for the Makaha lot and some cash to build a house. I will move to Makaha and live there."

My mother shifted her stance and continued, "Commuting to school every day will be difficult, so you girls can stay in town with your father during the school week and come to Makaha for weekends. I don't need a car during the week. Summer vacation will be here in a few months, and then you can move out full-time."

I assured my mother we would all be okay—I wanted the best for her. But I did not look forward to staying in town with my father during the school week. My mother was my anchor. For her sake, though, I was sure we would make it work.

She then walked deliberately to my father's workshop and asked him for a divorce. I imagine she was direct, saying something like, "It is time that you go your way and I go mine, with nothing in between." My father protested mildly. At first he seemed put out, disgruntled that my mother was asking to leave the marriage. It was as though he was offended that she would dare do this. He seemed to wonder why everyone—I think this might have included his new paramour, Anne—could not live as one happy family. When he brought up the idea of coexistence, my mother scotched it. "No way," she insisted. "I am going my way, and you need to go yours. Hopefully, our paths will not cross."

No matter what he said or did in the days that followed, my mother had made up her mind. She wanted nothing more of married life with him.

Leaving Waikiki

Two weeks later, at the end of January, Betty packed up and we all moved out of our house in Waikiki. She went to Makaha. My father rented a two-bedroom apartment near Diamond Head. Gloria and I balanced our week between the two places, calling ourselves city mice and country mice.

Makaha was definitely the country in the 1950s. There wasn't much traffic between Honolulu and the Westside, but the thirty-six mile drive took more than an hour. There was no regular public transportation, either. The only option was either driving your own car or taking one of the converted taxis that left every few hours from Chinatown. Filipino women drove the old sedans, and they were as tough as nails—cockfight gamblers and cigar smokers. Other than in an emergency, we avoided this option. My mother sold the Caddy, I sold my surf wagon, and she bought a VW bug that I drove back and forth to town. This left her without a car, but she didn't care. She was happy to be stranded at Makaha.

Family friends did gossip. Some of them thought Betty left Ron for surfing. Years later, I heard that a few friends and family members admired her for the courage to leave a life she was not happy with, and to forgo financial support for an uncertain future. Several friends, as well as my cousin, said they wished their mothers would show similar gumption.

During the time we stayed with my father, he often excoriated my mother and the Pembrokes. I never liked to hear these put-downs and wondered why he delivered them. Life was tense during this time of transition. But somehow we all managed to make it through the few months until school was out. I drove Gloria and myself back and forth to Makaha as much as possible, even though the commute was tough. To get to school, we left before 5:00 a.m. and arrived back home at dusk. It was a tedious, time-consuming drive, made more so by the ocean, which seemed to call me, beckoning with the excitement of surf life.

Since there had been nothing on our property besides the icehouse, Betty talked the Sumidas, our Waiʻanae-side neighbors, into renting her a Quonset hut that sat next to our lot. The Sumidas lived in Pearl City, where they were watercress farmers, and used the Quonset hut only for weekend fishing.

The two-room Quonset hut was rustic—and rusting. Its outdoor bathroom had only a toilet and sink. The cold-water shower was located in the front yard, next to the beach, under a hau tree. Because of the lack of privacy, we showered in the dark, after sundown or before dawn. This wasn't the only experience that was just this side of miserable. There were two sets of bunk beds on a plywood floor. One lightbulb dangled from the ceiling on a fraying electric cord. For meals, we cooked on a two-burner Coleman camp stove, and stored food in a small, rusty refrigerator. But it was a roof over our head until Betty could get a house built. In spite of the living situation, my mother seemed elated. She surfed every morning and started planning the home she would construct on her beach lot.

On February 5, 1959, the Makaha property was transferred into my mother's name. Over the next month, she got the cash settlement from my father and ordered a Lindal Cedar home from the state of Washington.

During these early years, telephones were scarce at Makaha. They were expensive, so very few houses had a line. To stay in touch with us, my mother would call at night from the Klausmeyers', our other neighbors on the Kaʻena Point side. One night, she started her conversation by saying, "Act like everything is fine, and don't tell your father what I'm going to tell you. Today I had a little accident; a surfboard hit me behind my right knee and caused a hematoma. I managed to get a ride to the ʻEwa Plantation Hospital." The hospital was twenty miles away, but, fortunately, our friend Dr. Wall was in charge. "Dr. Wall performed surgery and drained the hematoma. I have a few stitches in my leg. Don't worry, I'm fine, and Dr. Wall is taking extra-good care of me. In fact, he just brought me a martini and dinner. Tomorrow he'll drive me back home to Makaha."

In her years of surfing, Mother had many "little" accidents, including several that bruised and/or broke her ribs, leaving her with pain and discomfort. The injuries never dampened her spirit and love for the sport. She handled these mishaps, as well as other stumbling blocks, with her usual cool.

Mishaps or not, my mother, Gloria, and I got along well and had a happy coexistence in the Quonset hut. Surfing friends dropped by, and we enjoyed evenings together. My mother had a knack for creative cooking and wasn't perturbed by the limitations of two burners. The time in the Quonset hut did bring out her austere habits, though. She used every bit of food in the refrigerator, so there was nothing to throw away. If there were four people to feed, she made salad for three and a half. One day she saw a speck of what looked like meat in the kitchen sink drain. She picked it up and put it in her mouth, but quickly spat it out. My sister and I realized what she had done: She had eaten cat food. We all had a good laugh over that incident.

In the summer, Mother traded the Volkswagen bug for a Kombi bus so that she could haul house materials. This bus was also perfect for an occasional surf trip to the North Shore. After surfing one afternoon, George Downing invited us on the spur of the moment to Henry Preece's birthday party in Haleʻiwa. It was a local-style party gathering with Hawaiian music, plenty of food, beer, and homemade pineapple swipe, eighty-proof liquor made from fermenting pineapple. Mother drove back home to Makaha after the party, following the dirt road around Kaʻena Point. The road was carved out beside abandoned railroad tracks, and in places we looked down over thirty-foot-high cliffs as the full moon made the ocean shimmer.

Mother had also made friends with some of the locals and was beginning to create her own social life. Some men emerged on the scene, but after the treacherous years with my father, Betty was cool on the idea of another man until the right one came along. She always enjoyed male company and was only attracted to men who were creative, talented, and doing things. They were also attracted to Betty.

A House of Her Own

Betty had worked hard for twenty-five years to help Ron build the jewelry business, but she was barely able to get enough cash out of the divorce to build a house, buy furnishings, and have a financial cushion. My father

Betty showing off her coordination, strength,
and athleticism in her late 40's

Betty's Lindal Cedar Home on the beach with the Makaha Valley
and Majestic Wai'anae Mountain Range in the backdrop, 1959

immediately changed the locks on the shop in the Alexander Young
Building at Bishop and Hotel Streets. Betty thought this was a low blow,
denying her entry to the family business, but she moved on. When the
dust settled, she would figure out how to get her workbench, tools, personal belongings, and materials back into her possession.

Betty turned her attention to building her house. She found a prefabricated model that suited her, but, despite numerous trips to the building
permitting office in Honolulu, bureaucrats stalled. It was the late '50s; she
was a haole and a woman. They didn't take her seriously. They were also
unfamiliar with kit homes. Betty believed their thinking lacked creativity.

One day, after many visits to the permitting office, Betty walked out
frustrated, perplexed, and almost in tears. Outside the door, walking up
the sidewalk, she spotted one of surfing buddies, the photographer Clarence Maki. It turned out that Clarence was an outside building inspector
who worked with the men who were giving her a bad time. After Betty
explained her problems, Clarence put his arm around her shoulder and
said, "We are going to fix this." He walked her back into the office and
introduced Betty. "This lady is a surfing champion, and I want you guys
to give her a building permit right now," Clarence said. That did it.

Prefabricated houses were still new. Lindal Cedar Homes had been founded in 1945, and this was only fourteen years later. Betty's own house was made of tongue-and-groove cedar and cost around $10,000. She acted as her own contractor and oversaw every stage of building, which included installing the framing and constructing the roof. She worked alongside the carpenters, doing as much as possible, as they assembled the frame and put together the precut lumber for walls. In June, after the roof was on, we moved into the shell. Over the next six months, Betty bought plumbing fixtures and other inside materials at a discount store and schlepped them to Makaha. She rented a tile cutter and finished the kitchen counter and sink with a mosaic of broken pink tiles. She used the same pink mosaic on the backsplash but embedded three black, surfing stick figures. She tiled the bathrooms, laid the linoleum flooring, and stained the outside and inside walls. She even made several clever hanging light fixtures.

Betty working at her handmade surf inspired tile sink

The lasting impression of her family's Depression-era difficulties meant that Betty paid cash for everything she bought and never incurred a mortgage on her Makaha property. True to her lifelong desire for a "strongbox," Betty locked the past twenty-five years behind her. She had vowed early on that that she would always be able to support herself, and she knew that her skill in dental hygiene would still be there if she needed it.

From a young age, I had my own ideas and was independent, not an easy child to parent. But Betty was the perfect mother for me. In high school, when my friends were having trouble with their parents, my mother provided a safe and happy haven for all in Makaha. Most of my friends wanted to be at our house with my mother, wishing their own mothers could be like Betty.

"One night we arrived at her house after dark," remembers my high school surfing buddy Jan Lee. "My car had broken down. We hid our boards in some bushes and hitchhiked around Ka'ena Point to Makaha from Sunset Beach. We knocked at the door, and Betty opened it. She asked us if we had eaten (no) and without a second's hesitation invited us to have dinner and spend the night. I learned a lot of things at Betty's Makaha house: about eating, surfing, and just plain sharing. Plus, Betty loved nature. She taught me to do the same."

CHAPTER 10

SOJOURN IN SOUTH AMERICA (1960)

When Betty was in Lima in 1956, she told friends at Club Waikiki about surfing with her daughter. I had met some of the Peruvian friends when they visited Hawaii, and loved their vivacious view of life. They mostly all had magnanimous personalities—personalities that not only lit up a room but ignited a social situation. As an avid and aspiring surfer, I thought it would be a dream come true to travel to Peru. My mother had dangled the possibility before me, but she had had a condition: I had to win the Makaha International Surfing Championships. After I did so in November 1957, the invitation was clinched. I graduated from high school in June 1959, and we would travel to Lima in January 1960, as a mother-daughter surfing team.

When my father heard of our plans, he flexed his domineering muscles and told my mother she could not take me out of the country. Honolulu was still a small town, and, through what was known as the coconut wireless, it was hard to keep certain secrets. My mother was afraid that if we got our passports in Honolulu, my father would find out and then concoct a way to prevent us from traveling. But I was eighteen, and my mother promised me that we were going to Lima no matter what. The previous year, through mutual friends, Betty had been introduced to David, who was a visitor to Hawaii from San Francisco. They had had a brief romance, so we planned a vacation around a trip to San Francisco, ostensibly to see relatives. We flew to California, stayed with David for a few days, visited some Pembrokes, and picked up our passports. Then we flew to Mexico City and on to Lima. David was nice but a city man and basically not my mother's type, as he couldn't build anything or catch any fish. That was the end of that.

I don't know why Ron made such a fuss over our trip. Only two months after the divorce, he had married Anne Lamont, with whom he had been cavorting while he and my mother were still married. He still spoke of leaving the islands, but Anne loved Hawaii. She helped him with work, and he shuttled between his apartment in Waikiki and the jewelry business in downtown Honolulu. (Eventually, he bought land in Arizona and on the Big Island, but age set in before he managed to make a move to either, and he never realized his dream.)

With Gloria, it was more complicated. My mother, sister, and I usually traveled in tandem. But Gloria was only sixteen, still in high school, and had to stay behind. She seemed closer in spirit to my father than I was, so we didn't think she would mind. Luckily, Anne took Gloria under her wing and they bonded.

My mother and I focused on the role that was given us. We had been invited as guests of Club Waikiki to promote surfing among women. Peru was a socially conservative country, but Club Waikiki's male members wanted to encourage their wives and girlfriends to surf. The women were hesitant, as they considered it a masculine sport. Our job was to surf, have fun, be feminine, and generate interest. We traveled to the club every day. The water was not at all like Hawaii's—it was never clear and had a distinctly icky smell, but it was still great to be there. (We may have given surf culture in Peru a boost—a lot of women surf there today. In fact, one Peruvian woman became a professional women's surfing champion in 2004: Sofia Mulánovich won the world title at five feet, four inches and 121 pounds.)

As with Betty's first trip, the Peruvians tapped us into their social circle, hosting us for dinners at special restaurants and for parties at the club. They treated us like celebrities, bestowing upon us flower bouquets, a silver plaque with our names engraved, and gold jewelry. Club Waikiki hosted an annual luau in our honor, and I was made "queen" of the party. My name was added to the surfboard plaque, on the original board from Duke Kahanamoku, as the fourth reina del luau. (The tradition continued through the 1990s.)

Betty and Vicky as the guest of honor for the
Club Waikiki party in Lima, Peru, 1960

Cesar Barrios paid for a fifth-floor apartment in a quaint building in downtown Lima. It was not glamorous, but it was spacious and comfortable, with a kitchen, sitting room, and bedroom overlooking the city and the University of San Marcos. Smells of food cooking in the streets drifted up to our flat from down below. There was a funky elevator with a small, skinny, and ancient operator who greeted us every meeting with "*Buenos días, señoras.*" We tried to have conversations but didn't get too far with him, given our limited Spanish.

Some nights we could hear yelling from the students rioting at the nearby university. This was the beginning of the movement that later became known as the Shining Path. We often smelled tear gas from mounted police who were attempting to control the rioting.

The political activism around us did nothing to discourage us from turning into social butterflies. We packed every day with activities, almost every night with outings. Evenings when we did not socialize with our Peruvian friends, we strolled in the direction opposite the university to the central historic district, just a few blocks away, and often sought out a low-key Peruvian restaurant for dinner. We fell in love with *anticuchos*, seafood stews, chicken grilled on a spit, ceviche, and other savory dishes.

One evening after our meal, we walked back to our apartment, admiring the illumination on the historic buildings. The life-size statues of Peruvian heroes decorated the plazas, and the fountains were alive with colored light rays dancing to the rhythms of Latin music. We strolled across the Plaza San Martín, passing a statue of a mounted Francisco Pizarro. (The Spanish conquistador conquered Peru in 1532.) We walked toward the five-story Hotel Bolivar, built in 1924, the first modern hotel in Lima. It was a glamorous architectural gem that attracted famous people and Hollywood movie stars during the 1940s and '50s, such as Orson Welles, Ava Gardner, and John Wayne. Mother knew it well, as she and the Hawaiian surfing team members had stayed there on her first trip to Lima.

"Let's go have a drink and see who's inside," she said. We were dressed for the occasion, Betty in a navy-blue sheath and I in a white sundress. We stepped through the glass entry door into a lobby with ornate, multitiered chandeliers that hung from twenty-foot-high ceilings. The chairs and couches were upholstered in Italian tapestry. We walked down burgundy-carpeted stairs to the Grill Bolivar, which was dimly lit and exuded old-world elegance. We smelled cigars and cognac.

The maître d' escorted us to a burgundy velvet booth. Mother scooted in first, then patted the seat, welcoming me to join her. I scooted up close to her. We felt like royalty in the European-style cabaret. We spoke softly and chuckled as the waiter arrived with two pisco sours. The hotel was famous for Peru's national drink of brandy, lime juice, bitters, syrup, and egg whites. Soon, violins began to play the lilting notes of "Romantica," which had just been voted Italy's song of the year. Today, all these years later, I can still hear the singer and strings playing that haunting song.

As we lifted our glasses for the first sip, Mother called out, "*Hola! Buenas noches!*" I looked over to see two men we had recently met at the club, the sons of Cesar Barrios, who had taken a special interest in us. It seemed like a magical coincidence. Cesar's sons joined us in the booth and we talked about surfing and life in Hawaii for hours. We parted ways with hugs and kisses, saying, "See you at the club."

My mother and I picked our way gingerly along the cobblestones on our alley, which was bordered by an eight-foot wall. The romance of the setting was usually dashed by the sight of twenty mounted policemen lining our street, monitoring the rioting students, along with the inevitable smell of horses and urine. After our late night at Grill Bolivar, neither horse manure nor agitated youth prevented us from feeling as if we were in heaven.

The Top of the World

As if that heaven weren't enough, we also took a trip to the top of the world—or at least the top of the Andes. We flew to Cuzco, one of the oldest inhabited cities in the western hemisphere, and spent a few days sightseeing in the old colonial town, which was once the capital of the Inca empire. The cold mountain air was filled with a pungent, smoky smell from woodburning stoves used for cooking and heating. We were both in awe of the stonework; ancient rocks weighing tons fit together so tightly that a butter knife could not penetrate the seams. Inca descendants trudged along the old cobblestone streets, hauling heavy loads on their backs, their cheeks bulging with coca leaves.

A few days later, we took the day train to Machu Picchu, the fabled lost city of the Incas. We were the only Americans in a car full of French travelers. We befriended Henri Hervet, a bombardier and World War I hero who owned two banks, one near the Loire Valley at Bourges and another in Paris. We spent the day walking with him around the ruins. (Ten years later, I spent an unforgettable month in Paris as the guest of Henri and his family.)

On a separate adventure, we took a trip on the world's second-highest railroad, the Ferrocarril Central del Péru. We ascended to an altitude of 15,608 feet, through desolate mining towns in the Andes. We traveled through Ticlio, one of the highest traveled mountain passes in the world, and, after eight hours of crossing high bridges and dark tunnels, we arrived in Huancayo, famous for its Indian market. Colorful handmade treasures spilled out of simple stalls: woven blankets, baskets, pottery, crafts, fruits, and vegetables. We spent two full days wandering around the pre-Columbian town with a friend from the club who acted as our personal guide.

Finally, after six weeks, it was time for my mother to return to Hawaii to work. I loved life in Lima and decided to stay. I took a job as a companion for a young English girl, Janet Lawson, who lived with her father in a hilly sun-belt town, Chosica, forty-five minutes outside Lima. The Lawsons had servants to do all the cooking, cleaning, housekeeping, and yard work, so Janet and I did not lift a finger. It was an easy life and a lovely place to work, but I became bored. Winter rolled around, and the coast became overcast and dismal, which ended the surfing days at Club Waikiki. I had the use of a car and drove it to spend weekends in Lima with Rosalba and Carlos Rey, but most other members headed to their mountain club, Los Condores. Isolated and homesick for Hawaii, I was ready to leave Peru.

CHAPTER 11

LIFE AFTER LIMA (1961–63)

When Betty returned to Hawaii, she started to look for work as a dental hygienist. Over the years, she had kept up her California license, but that was not enough for Hawaii. To practice there, she would need to take a test and get a license. So, for the interim, she landed a job at Hickam Air Force Base, working for a dentist, Dr. Mauer, for more than a year, until she could get her Hawaii license. Soon Dr. Mauer was out of the military and hired Betty as a hygienist to work in his private practice. (Over the following years, she also worked part-time for other dentists.)

In the fall of 1960, Gloria returned to Punahou, I entered the University of Hawaii, and Betty rented an apartment in Honolulu. I was conflicted between what I *should* do and what I *wanted* to do. I knew I needed an education, but part of me still wanted to surf. In a way, we all wanted to stay at Makaha, but going to school seemed like the thing to do. Punahou was a college prep school, and I, like everyone else there, was expected to head for college. Most of my classmates from Punahou had gone to prestigious mainland colleges. I felt stuck at the University of Hawaii, which was not a friendly place for a haole girl during those years; most of the students were Japanese and kept to their own cliques.

111

A saving grace was that our friend, the big-wave surfer Peter Cole, agreed to be my algebra tutor. I still did poorly in math. (Not his fault.)

Betty, too, had her mind on Makaha. She started to cook up various schemes for starting a small business so she could live there full-time. At one point, she entertained the idea of backing Pat Curren, the big-wave surfer and master board shaper, in a surfboard-making business, but the fact that Pat mostly wanted to surf and hang out meant there was little guarantee that this would be a profitable venture. Another idea was to run a small fat farm for women who wanted to lose weight and get healthier. She imagined booking a few women at a time and having them sprint on the beach, kick furiously in the ocean, and eat salads and fish. Another whim was to open a bar and restaurant with Jim Arness. At the time, the star of the popular television series *Gunsmoke* was a frequent visitor to Makaha. He loved surfing, preferring Makaha to other breaks, and had become a close friend. Jim offered to be a silent partner, but Betty was told that getting a liquor license would involve bribes and paybacks to the local mob, known as the Syndicate. She decided she had better stick to dentistry.

More Building

Living and working in two places was expensive and led Betty to yet another scheme. She had long had plans for what she called a garage on the street side of the property. She built it, and after the building inspectors signed off, she turned it into a studio. The four-hundred-square-foot space was built with black cinder blocks, wood, and glass. One wall of the studio was open to a four-foot-wide tropical garden bordered by a six-foot-high lava-rock wall. Ferns, ti, ginger, and heliconia plants grew in the dirt between the studio and the wall, which continued and curved around the studio on the ocean side, sheltering an outdoor shower and small bathroom. The roof over the entire garden was a heavy metal mesh screen that allowed sun and rain to fall on the outdoor "room." Here, she could live happily on weekends, make jewelry, do lab work when necessary, and rent the house to make ends meet.

For a few years, Jim Arness had been renting Jimmy Wong's house, next door on the Kaʻena side, for his surf vacations. Although he was then famous as Marshal Matt Dillon, to us Jim was really just another surfer pal and, at six feet, seven inches, an especially tall and charismatic one. While I was a senior in high school, Jim and I even stayed in touch via letters. My English teacher, Mr. Metcalf, loved *Gunsmoke* and waxed on endlessly about it in class. I sat there silent but secretly thrilled. On my way home from Peru, I spent the summer in Coronado and Jim invited me to join the *Gunsmoke* gang (Dolly, Chester, and others) in their box seats at the Del Mar horse races. After the event, we all went to a German chalet restaurant in Del Mar where we drank beer, listened to accordion music, ate sauerbraten, and visited. It was an exciting evening for a starry-eyed eighteen-year-old. Several men approached our table, wanting to meet Jim, who hurriedly said hello and gave me a less starry-eyed insight into the life of a celebrity. A few weeks later, Jim toured me around the *Gunsmoke* film location, the Hollywood Hills, and his ranch in Simi Valley, where his father lived. In Westwood, we bought books and Gauguin art prints from a local bookstore. Jim was much more than a cowboy surfer.

Our friendship with Jim had grown over the next few years, and he became one of Betty's first tenants in the main house. He typically arrived with a gang of family and friends, and they quickly melded with life in Makaha. One day Betty told Jim, "You have to meet Buffalo Keaulana and his wife, Momi." She then walked him down the beach to where Buff and Momi lived in an upstairs cottage above the lifeguard station. Buffalo was eating fish and poi and offered some to Jim. Years later, Buff told me about tricking Jim that day with a bottle of chili water used to spice the fish and poi. Buff held his thumb over the opening and pretended to drink straight from the bottle. Jim, not wanting to be outdone, grabbed the bottle, tipped it up to his mouth, and drank half of the chili water. His eyes filled with tears and turned red, while his mouth burned from the heat. Everyone laughed hysterically, and Jim ate the whole bowl of poi to put out the fire. Jim forgave Buffalo. In fact, the occasion seemed to cement the friendship between the two and they were life-long friends.

Jim always invited Betty over to the house to have Long John Silvers (rum with a cocktail mix). These would often be followed by a barbecue and the occasional prank. Jim loved Makaha: the surf, the life, and the beauty, particularly the spectacular full moons over the Wai'anae mountains. As the pearl-gold sphere peeked over the ridge and then kept rising behind Mount Ka'ala, Jim and his friends would stand on the porch and howl like coyotes. Hawaiian-kine coyotes.

After her weekend cottage was erected, Betty talked the Sumidas, her neighbors on the 'Ewa side, into letting her replace their rickety Quonset hut with a pair of two-bedroom, prefab round houses. Betty loved building projects, but this was also a way to improve the neighborhood. She ordered the houses, got the permits, oversaw the construction, and did some of the finish work herself.

"Betty always seemed to be involved in some kind of home-improvement project that, until then, we had only seen men tackle," Barbara Sumida told me. She was a child when Betty built the cottages for her family. "She did carpentry and plumbing, worked with ceramic tile, and built a lava-rock shower stall. I could tell by the way she showed us her projects that she loved doing this work. Other times, I would find Betty at her workbench, carefully crafting a piece of fine jewelry with the most delicate tools. She seemed to do these things in a natural, fun way that invited us to follow. Her verve was a gift Betty offered to everyone she knew. I have tried to take that with me."

Betty found other ways to express her unconventionality. She had not lost her fascination with fast cars. Gloria and I lived mostly in town, while Betty drove back and forth to and from Makaha. To make the commute to her new jobs in Honolulu bearable, she bought a silver-blue Corvette. She happily raced back and forth to Honolulu in it, dodging policemen along the way. (Betty's daredevil driving didn't stop. In the summer of 1970, my daughters, Marcie and Rennie, were eight and nine years old when they spent a month with my mother. During a ride to visit their paternal grandmother in Honolulu, Betty asked, "Girls, have you ever gone one hundred miles an hour in an automobile? Do you want to see what it feels like to go that fast?" They squealed, "Yes, let's go that fast! Please, Tutu, let's go." Betty then put her foot to the pedal. Rennie remembers seeing 100 on the speedometer.)

Over a ten-year period, Betty's Corvette was a major source of plea-sure. Eventually, though, she tired of getting speeding tickets. The thrill was not worth the expense. Also, some neighborhood kids were putting sand in her gas tank. She decided to get less conspicuous wheels and bought a two-door black Cadillac Seville. She was also growing weary of working in dental hygiene—leaning over people, cleaning dirty teeth in mouths struggling to stay open. She wanted to do more creative work. She decided to start her own dental laboratory to make custom porcelain bridges and dentures. She dove in, confident that even at age sixty she had the manual dexterity, dental background, and abundant self-confidence to master the craft.

Through USC Extension in Los Angeles, she took classes like Full Mouth Rehabilitation Waxing Technique, Functional Oral Diagnosis, and Science of Occlusion. Certainly, the names of the classes would have made her surfing buddies howl. Occasionally, she flew to Los Angeles and other mainland cities for workshops and conferences. Betty met and became friends with Charlie Stewart, the former dean of the dental school at USC and a porcelain guru. Always a fast study, Betty found other experts in the field as well to mentor her.

Now, besides working as a part-time hygienist, Betty did custom porcelain work for several dentists in Honolulu. She used Dr. Mauer's office during off-hours for her lab. Later on, she rented her own office in the Alexander Young Building on Bishop and Hotel Streets, where, oddly, Ron still had his jewelry business. Betty worked into the wee hours, and many a night she slept on a futon there, but she fled to Makaha whenever she could.

The End of an Era

At this point, for both of us, new activities consumed our lives. Neither one of us had much time for surfing, though I suspect something deeper was at play. Betty had to work full-time to keep herself and the family afloat, and she poured her weekend energy into the finish work on her studio. By 1961, she was commuting to Honolulu to work as a dental hygienist and learning a new profession. And she was maintaining two residences, which took all her time in Makaha. Also, by now, she had suffered several small surfing accidents and was thinking that she couldn't afford to get hurt again. Then she fell in love with a fisherman. His name was Charlie, and he led her farther and farther out into the sea.

In my case, circumstances had also dimmed my passion—an event on Veterans' Day, November 11, 1959. On several occasions, surfers from California camped out at our house until they found a more permanent residence. For three weeks, Frank Brandley, a fairly novice surfer from Coronado, had been staying with us while he learned to surf Makaha. In California, Frank had hung out with a group of older Coronado surfers and had decided to drop out of community college in San Diego to surf in Hawaii. Stories of the winter waves at Makaha and Sunset Beach had lured him. Being nineteen, Frank was also soul searching, trying to find his place in life. While at our house, he hatched the idea of staying in Hawaii and entering the University of Hawaii to study marine biology.

Frank wrote several letters home to his parents, telling them about his interest in Gloria. She was still no surfer, but she had become enamored of Frank, an admiral's son who was six feet tall and handsome, with blue eyes and loose brown hair. The three of us decided to go to Hale'iwa to join some other friends from California. On the afternoon of November 10th, I drove us in my surf wagon around Ka'ena Point, on its deeply pocked dirt road. On the North Shore, we met up with Tom Keck, John Elwell, and Tom Carlin.

By the time we found them, at Hale'iwa Beach Park, it was nearing dusk. We made a fire, cooked dinner, watched the sun drop below the western horizon, and gathered around, telling stories and talking about how great the surf would be in the morning. We all camped out; I slept in my surf wagon. In the morning, we woke up early and hit the six-foot surf that was cranking out off the jetty at Ali'i Beach. Everything seemed perfect. Frank was an inexperienced surfer but believed he was ready for these conditions and caught some waves. We were all having a great time. I was sitting outside, waiting for a set. Frank caught a couple of rides and was paddling back out close to the incoming break. Too close. Tom Keck and John Elwell were riding in the critical part, with the wave breaking just behind them. Frank stopped paddling and was watching them, spellbound, but he was in the direct path of the surfers, who were unable to avoid him. Frank didn't know to get under his board for protection and was hit in the head and knocked unconscious. He floated on top of the water for a few seconds, before disappearing under the next wave.

The surfers Tom and John yelled, "Frank is under! We've got to get him!"

No one had a face mask, and the waves kept coming, churning the area with turbulence and spewing white water, making a search almost impossible. For endless moments, we experienced a helpless, horrible feeling, knowing he was so close yet so far. Other surfers came over and dove down, trying to find Frank with their bare eyes.

I paddled in to shore to find a pay phone and called the fire department. There were several rings before anyone answered. I screamed into the phone, "A surfer has been hit by a board. He's disappeared underwater. We need help. Please hurry."

The out-of-shape search-and-rescue team from the Waialua Fire Department finally showed up and seemed almost afraid to go in the water. But by this time, at least half an hour after Frank had sunk into the churning sea, Bud Browne had dived down and pulled Frank's body to the shore. Buzzy Trent appeared and did mouth-to-mouth resuscitation. A fireman also tried to resuscitate Frank, but their resuscitator broke down. It was hopeless. We stood around, in shock at first, and then quietly lamented the loss of this young man, our new friend. Gloria and I drove back to Makaha feeling like our hearts had been ripped out. This was a pivotal incident in my life and one I have thought about every November 11th for the past sixty years.

I never felt the same about surfing again.

CHAPTER 12

BECOMING A FISHERWOMAN (1963–89)

After divorcing Ron Heldreich, Betty settled into her own identity as a single woman. She built a house, a studio, two round houses, and a dental lab. She befriended lifeguard Buffalo Keaulana and Marshal Matt Dillon. She saw her daughters start to forge lives of their own. In 1962, I had left UH, married a Punahou classmate and boyfriend, Ron Durand, and moved to San Jose, California. Gloria graduated from high school in 1963. That same year, while Betty was working for Dr. Mauer, a patient and friend told her she just had to meet Charlie Winstedt, a building contractor who was crafting a fifty-five-foot fishing boat.

Betty and her friend went to the construction yard to see the boat, which Charlie was trying to finish so he could go deep-sea fishing. Betty and Charlie struck up an animated conversation. Liking work she could do with her hands, Betty offered to help. He took her up on the proposition. The following week, every day after work, she met him to sand, paint, or do whatever was needed to get the boat in the water. In time, she and Charlie started going out to dinner after they finished for the day. Soon they were dating. Betty was impressed with Charlie, as he seemed so inventive and smart.

When Charlie was one year old, his father had come to Hawaii from Sweden to build the Aloha Tower, a Honolulu Harbor landmark, which was completed in 1926. Charlie had not gone to college, because World War II closed down the schools, even Punahou, where Charlie was a student. But he made up for this by reading extensively. Being an autodidact suited him. He was an inventor and a man capable of building anything from low-end bungalows to high-rise apartment buildings and fishing boats.

At six foot two, Charlie was a hunky man with dancing blue eyes. Born with a genetic condition that gave him droopy eyelids, he was nevertheless a happy and kind person who liked to socialize.

After all the final finishing work was done, Charlie named his boat *Kuu Huapala* (*My Sweetheart*). The sampan was built for big-game sport fishing, and Betty joined Charlie on three-to-four-day trips to Molokai, Maui, the Big Island, Kauai, and Necker Island. They would return with coolers of seafood. In 1969, on their way home from Niihau, Charlie caught a 210-pound ahi off the Wai'anae Coast that was as tall as he was. After another fishing trip, the *Honolulu Star-Bulletin* published an article that referred to him as a marlin "marauder."

Betty and Charlie Windstedt fishing off of Moloka'i

Betty had slowly stopped surfing. She did not have enough time or energy to work in both Honolulu and Makaha, learn a new career, and maintain properties. Then she had also met Charlie and fallen in love. Betty the surfer woman became a fishing woman. Charlie was smitten, but he had gotten out of an unpleasant first marriage several years before meeting Betty and was hesitant about entering another committed relationship. He often palled around with his friend Kenneth, who was in the steel business, taking trips to Japan with him and visiting bars and bathhouses. At first, Betty was usually available for whatever Charlie wanted to do. But even after six years of dating, Charlie remained evasive about the question of marriage. Betty loved Charlie, wanted a committed relationship, and was growing tired of the status quo. Meanwhile, another Charlie, in California, was showing some interest. Betty decided it was time to force Charlie Winstedt's hand.

His and Hers Shops

By then, I was living with my own family in Montecito, in a wood cottage south of Santa Barbara. Mother rented out her house in Makaha, shipped her Corvette to California, found a job working for a dentist in Santa Barbara, and started dating Charlie Stewart. During the week, she slept in our living room on a hide-a-bed. Betty saw Charlie Stewart at night and on weekends. Barely a month had passed before Hawaii Charlie boarded a plane, came to California, and proposed.

Charlie Winstedt had already made Betty the second mate on his boat. He decided to make her the first mate in his life. They were married in 1968 in Las Vegas. After a honeymoon in California, they returned to Hawaii. They were both in their late fifties. They soon retired, lived at Makaha, and threw themselves into building projects.

Together, Betty and Charlie could make anything. They spent years working on the house, redesigning porches, redoing floors and windows, building a redwood *furo*—a Japanese-style soaking tub—and adding a second two-car garage to the side of the house (since Betty had turned the first one into a studio). After a while, Charlie figured they needed a place to store tools and complete work projects. The icehouse, our original camp house, was taken away. Charlie oversaw the building of "his and hers" shops in its place. Into his shop, he brought a multitude of woodworking tools, including a lathe. He turned beautiful wooden bowls and plates of all sizes. To her shop, Betty added a darkroom. Already an avid photographer, she processed color and black-and-white prints there. She also made rings, pins, and charms for friends and family.

During the 1970s, after several years living at Makaha and commuting to Honolulu for fishing, Betty and Charlie decided driving back and forth to town was wasting gas, money, and time. They sold the *Kuu Huapala* and replaced it with a more manageable, twenty-six-foot fishing boat they could keep in the backyard.

They trailered this boat behind their white jeep to Pokai Bay, just a few miles down the road. This made fishing off the Wai'anae Coast fairly easy. They usually caught plenty. Betty discovered all sorts of ways to eat their catch, ranging from ahi sashimi to cioppino, fried mahi-mahi, ono tempura, and menpachi steamed Chinese-style over watercress. Friends came over for evenings of cocktails, fish dinners, and fun.

To Vancouver on the *Maui Lu*

In 1980, Betty and Charlie heard about a trip from Maui to Canada on a 131-foot diesel ship called the *Maui Lu*. It was a luxury yacht with seven staterooms and five heads, owned by an old friend of Betty's, a rough-and-tumble lumber tycoon named Gordon Gibson. Gibson had served in Parliament and was known in Canada as the Bull of the Woods. Gordon and his first wife, Lou, had been jewelry customers since the Waikiki days.

In the early 1950s, Gordon had bought twenty-eight acres on Maui in Kihei, then a strip of gorgeous white-sand beach and a town that was mostly scrubby kiawe trees and a scattering of little wooden shacks. The Gibsons built a resort called the Maui Lu and split their time between Vancouver and Kihei. Betty would fly over and spend a few days of rest and recuperation at the resort with the Gibsons.

Before meeting Charlie, Betty vacationed with old friend,
Gordon Gibson, at the Gibson's resort in K'hei, Maui

Gordon was a big bear of a man. Betty respected him for his accomplishments and capabilities. He was her kind of guy. Lou died in 1967, just a few years after Betty met Charlie, but she and Gordon remained friends. Later, the three became friends, as Gordon and Charlie were similar.

Gordon's yacht had been harbored on Maui for many years. In 1974, Gordon, now in his eighties, and his second wife, Gertrude, wanted to take the ship back to Vancouver. Word got out that Gordon was looking for a crew. Before giving the trip too much thought, Betty signed on as the cook and Charlie as the second mate. They packed, flew to Maui, and spent a few days preparing for the 2,322-mile, eleven-day voyage to Canada.

On the afternoon of the boat's scheduled departure, May 16, 1974, their sendoff was celebrated with a luau in Kihei. The party was put on in grand Hawaiian style, with a lot of drinking, food, and merriment. Gordon, ever the prankster, decided to pull anchor just at dusk and depart in the middle of the celebration. The channel off Maui is one of the roughest in the world, and the minute the ship pulled out of the mooring, the seas turned turbulent. Water ran over the decks, and most of the crew was soon seasick.

That was not the only inauspicious moment. On the sixth night, the ship started taking on water in the engine room. Gordon first suspected a one-inch-wide, two-foot-long gash, patched with canvas, on the hull of the ship. Several scary hours passed before anyone could stop the water intake. Halfway between Hawaii and Canada, the crew thought they were going to sink to the bottom of the ocean. Turns out, the engineer had forgotten to close two valves when he started the bilge pumps, and water had gushed in. The battery was used up in the process of pumping the water out, which left no electricity and no refrigeration for the last five days of the trip.

Seasick and suffering from bronchitis, Betty cooked up all the food before it spoiled. The crew spent each night in darkness, which added to the gloom. Yet once they reached land and recovered, they all described the harrowing voyage as the experience of a lifetime. As Gordon put it, "It was the challenge of taking a risk and still being alive to tell the story."

Later, Gordon wrote gleefully in his book, *The Gordon Gibson Story*, that they had faced "the kind of seas that wear a man down." As time went on, Betty was inclined to describe it as a miserably cold, wet, eleven-day folly.

More relaxed trips followed, though, to New Zealand, Fiji, and the Great Barrier Reef in Australia. Charlie was obsessed with salmon fishing. Every summer for eight or nine years, they traveled to Canada. Charlie's goal was to be admitted into the prestigious Tyee Club, which required catching a chinook salmon weighing thirty pounds or more in the waters of the Campbell River. On the fourth or fifth trip, he finally made it. The weather was usually overcast, but fishing was important to Charlie, so Betty went along on the trips, summer after summer. Visiting their many friends in Canada made the cold and wet more bearable.

Last Projects

Charlie was caring and kind to my mother, as well as to my sister and me. He almost always had an insightful comment and took delight in entertaining us, reciting limericks with a twinkle in his eye. One of our favorites involved a cricket, a grasshopper, a game of tag, and a stubbed toe. Charlie was intelligent, creative, and inventive. The word "stepfather" is not warm enough to describe the comfort we felt with him, and we appreciated the endearing friendship and love Charlie and Betty had for each other. (My daughters later told me they always listened from their beds to hear the two smooching each other good night.)

Charlie was diagnosed with Parkinson's disease in 1975 and became increasingly immobile by the 1980s. The long-term degenerative disorder affects the central nervous system and results in symptoms—shaking, rigidity, slowness, and difficulty walking—that generally come on slowly but eventually disable the patient.

Parkinson's didn't stop Charlie from working with Betty on small projects. They fabricated a two-foot-long pot out of sheet copper for steaming a fish. It turned out beautifully and inspired them to start a foundry for casting large metal pots, brass hinges, doorknobs, dolphins, and other art objects. To heat the metal, they made a burner with bricks, using wood as the heating source. Needing higher temperatures, they bought a propane metal-heating unit. They proceeded with this work until Charlie conceded that he was too shaky to work with molten metals.

When he could no longer swim in the ocean, Charlie and Betty decided to craft a homemade therapy pool. The backyard was almost solid coral, so they hired a crew to dig out a twenty-by-thirty-foot rectangular hole. Some Makaha friends, Mickey and Roy, helped line the rectangle with bricks and install a plastic liner. By this time, Charlie was having trouble walking, so he often orchestrated the work party from a motorized cart he used to get around. Since the house was raised, he designed a plywood ramp that allowed him to drive the cart down from the kitchen door. Soon, Charlie and Betty had a bona fide swimming pool.

Both of them seemed determined to outwit fate. In time, there were falls. Charlie broke his hip. Always trying to conserve money, Betty refused any help, despite how tough a job taking care of a two-hundred-pound man was. At the end, she fed him, often losing her own appetite. Her physical and mental strength carried her through these sad times, but the caregiving took a toll.

Charlie died in a hospital bed in the living room in 1989, after twenty-five years with Betty. She called them the best years of her life.

> A treasured friendship
> Always to be remembered
> He lived life fully
>
> —Betty, 2008

CHAPTER 13

CHANGING TIDES (1990)

Betty took some time to rest, but then she traveled to the Galapagos Islands for a photographic safari. She took extensive pictures and videos of the sea life, and on the way home she visited old friends in Peru. Other travels included trips to visit Mickey and Roy. By now they had moved to the Southern Oregon coast with the forty-acre National Sand Dune Recreation Area in their back yard. In 1990 at age seventy-seven, Betty purchased her own red Honda ATV and the three raced each other around the dunes down to the beach for picnics.

After Betty's last travels, she returned to Makaha knowing that it was her true home. She had gone through her own life changes and watched the Westside change, too. They had become intertwined.

In the 1950s, when Betty first visited, the Wai'anae Coast was rural, with only a handful of residents. Wai'anae itself was a Hawaiian and Japanese agricultural town with an outdoor theater, two country markets, a hardware store, the M. Nii Tailor Shop, and a drugstore. The town had everything we needed and nothing more. There were a few small plantation houses, but Quonset huts from World War II dominated the neighborhoods. There were no streetlights, and the night skies were alive with constellations and shooting stars. This town had a certain charm,

Seventy-seven year old Betty on her ATV heading
for a day outing on the Oregon sand dunes, 1990.

and nature provided us with what we considered luxuries—especially the sandy beach and the endless ocean.

> Sixteen waterfalls
> Flowing with beauty and force
> Moving towards the sea
>
> —Betty, 2009

Makaha in the 1960s was even more remote than Waianae and offered a simple life: the ocean, the beach, full moons, and brilliant sunsets out over the sea, accompanied by the occasional mysterious and evasive green flash. During rainstorms, nine or more impressive waterfalls cascaded down the steep trenches on the valley walls behind our house. Afterward, there were rainbows everywhere. Our social company consisted mainly of friends visiting from Honolulu or the mainland.

During the late 1960s and '70s, as Charlie joined Betty in Makaha and they spent more and more time there, the area around them grew more densely populated, as lower-income families were pushed out to Waiʻanae or to other towns on the leeward side, where rents and property values were lower than in Honolulu. Waiʻanae and Makaha grew more developed and more diverse, but with a population that was more on the socioeconomic edge. About half the population of the coast at the time was native Hawaiian or part native Hawaiian. A 1978 report by Alu Like, a service agency dedicated to addressing the social and economic needs of the Hawaiian community, pointed out that many of the area's ills were rooted in an education system that suffered from a gap between local families and school administrations. Teachers were inexperienced and pedagogical methods ill suited to the resident population.

A 1979 article in the *Star-Bulletin* called the Waiʻanae Coast "a paradise with problems." Despite its rugged mountains, matchless beaches, and deep valleys, Sanford Zalburg wrote that the poverty level was double the average on Oahu, and one out of every three residents was getting some sort of assistance from the state Department of Social Services and Housing. "Jobs are scarce," Zalburg continued. "Kids come out of school unable to read and write well. There is a drug problem, a burglary problem, even the problem of suicide among the young. There are many kids who are alienated. They set brush fires. Sometimes they take out their frustration on school buildings, sometimes on haole tourists."

During these years, car rental companies and tourist guides warned visitors to avoid the Westside. Betty lived alone in the garage grotto, minding her own business, and had few or no problems. She had surfed with and befriended community leaders and local heavyweights. These surfers were respected and even feared, and they put the word out to leave her alone.

A few incidents did occur, like the time when three or four teenage boys were picking coconuts on the ocean side of the property. Betty went out and politely asked them to move along, telling them she wanted the coconuts for her own use. They ignored her and came farther onto the property, trying to knock the coconuts down from the tree. With that, she sprinted to the porch, grabbed a baseball bat, and sauntered over. The boys continued knocking coconuts out of the trees. Betty drew a line on the sandy ground and said, "I will knock your heads off if you come one step closer." They stopped, gave her the stink eye, murmured swear words, and walked off down the beach.

Betty would move back and forth between the garage and the house, and throughout this time had to face another kind of trouble: numerous tidal-wave warnings. Sirens would sound while police and Civil Defense paraded through the neighborhoods with megaphones, ordering everyone to evacuate their houses for higher ground. Betty always refused to leave. It wasn't just the inconvenience and the fear of vandalism—she really had nowhere to go. She would sit up all night in the living room and watch the water level on the horizon. In a tsunami, the more correct term adopted in the 1970s, the water has to go out before the destructive wave comes in. She had built her house up off the ground and fashioned it like a ship. It was forty feet back from the high-tide line, as the regulations required. She figured if the water came up during storms, it would pass right through the house, coming in the front and going on out the back. Things would be fine.

Makaha is essentially a half-mile-long, crescent-shaped cove. During most months, a large sand beach lay out in front of the house, and some years it measured as much as a hundred feet wide. The winter, north swell brings sand from the opposite side of Makaha to our side. The summer, south swell takes most all the sand back to the other end of the beach, exposing a large limestone shelf with rocks in front of the house. Betty took comfort from this shelf, believing it provided protection from high surf and hurricanes.

By the 1970s, Charlie had moved with her into the house. In November 1982, right before Thanksgiving, Hurricane 'Iwa bore down on the Hawaiian Islands with dangerously high winds. This time, Betty and Charlie and their dog, Moki, fled to the Makaha Inn. 'Iwa's track took it over the top of Kauai and west of Oahu, but it caused more than $250 million in damage. At Makaha, 'Iwa pushed the waves right up to the house, broke the front glass doors, and sent water all the way to the back of the lot. There was no electricity for days. The storm took down a small coconut tree in the front yard and made a mess of the house. But things were essentially fine after the extensive cleanup.

By the time of Hurricane Iniki, in 1992, Betty was solo again. But she was hardly alone. Throughout her fifty-five years of living at Makaha, old and new friends would stop by to see her, usually unannounced. My mother's social group included Ann and Wayne the Canadians, Judy the X-ray technician, Jose the Spaniard, Yen Sung and Ray the Chinese couple, and various others from the neighborhood, who traded cooking and favorite recipes. Others drove from Honolulu, even though city dwellers believe Makaha is located at the end of the earth. Betty loved this, saying that when she woke up in the morning, she never knew who and what the day would bring to her. Unlike Ron Heldreich, Charlie welcomed the company throughout their time together.

It was a good thing, because some of that company included family. I visited often with my girls, even living there in the early 1970s, and Gloria moved back in 1979. Gram Pembroke, who had lived with Cay and Ann after she separated from our grandfather in the late 1940s, spent her last few years in Makaha in the mid-1960s. Jane and Smithy moved down the beach at one point.

(Cay and Ann stayed in California, while Herbert ended up a gun-toting, restless cowboy working on ranches throughout California, Arizona,

Nevada, and New Mexico. After graduating from college, becoming a farrier, and marrying Beverly Daggs, the daughter of a lemon rancher, he had
a son and a daughter with her. But he roamed. He was possessed of a Robin
Hood philosophy, believing it was okay to take from the rich and give to
the poor. He was an avid reader, wrote poetry, loved my mother dearly,
and stayed distantly in touch with Betty through the years with letters. He
died in Albuquerque, New Mexico, in 1999, at the age of seventy-eight.)

One family legacy that Betty continued before, during, and after
Charlie was Makaha Halloween parties. Betty had fond memories of her
parents' extravagant parties in Salt Lake City. (Her mother's birthday
had been on Halloween and her father's the day afterward, so they had
had lavish adult celebrations with a lot of drinking and merriment.) She
made Halloween a celebration of her parents' memory. Each year she got
decked out in a different costume, usually wearing a moth-eaten wig from
her collection. There was a bonfire on the beach, with hot dogs and chili
beans. The first signs of the north swell often appeared at this time, and
Halloween was in a way linked to the idea that winter surf was on its way.

All of Betty's birthdays were celebrated in grand style with lots of family and
friends. This is an example of Betty's 85th birthday party with four generations
of family. Betty, center, with granddaughters Marcie and Rennie and great
grandsons Rhodes and Fritz. Behind them are Bob Liljestrand and Vicky.

Betty was a listener more than a talker, and she had a gift for making people feel important. My longtime friend Sheila Fletcher Kriemelman remembers, "There was a special light and lightness about her, a sense that she was all-knowing and wise in a shamanistic sense. She was curious about the world and about you, asking questions and making you feel like you were the most important person on the planet. Her memory was titanic—she would ask specifically about me, my work as an artist, and each member of my family, even if she hadn't seen them for years. Betty never whined, complained, or discussed her own woes; she was grateful for life, breath, and the present moment."

My mother believed in everyone's potential, whether they lived up to it or not. She connected with some people on a spiritual level and wanted to let them talk about what they were doing, rather than what she was doing. Soft-spoken and a woman of few words, Betty always had something meaningful to say. But that doesn't mean she was above being entertaining. She had a lot of personality and loved to clown around. She did a hilarious Donald Duck impression.

> Stop. It's five o'clock
> Time for fun and silly talk
> No arguing please
>
> —Betty, 2010

The Gracious Ladies of Surfing

There was one Makaha friendship that was special in its own way. Betty had first encountered Rell Sunn at the shore when Rell was seven. She watched as Rell became a serious waterwoman and the first native Hawaiian female to be hired by the city and county as a lifeguard on the Wai'anae Coast. She soon became known as the Queen of Makaha. In 1975, Rell founded the women's professional surfing tour and in 1982 ranked first in international professional surfing ratings. She helped organize the Women's Hui, the Women's Professional Surfing Association, and the Makaha Menehune Surf Meet, which for twenty-three years was an annual event benefiting at-risk children on the Westside. Rell's energy was endless, and, like Betty, she could change an everyday event into an adventure. *Surfing* magazine called her the Gracious Lady of Surfing; her story became the stuff of legend and the subject of the 2002 documentary film *Heart of the Sea*.

For years, Rell and Betty were essentially neighbors. When I lived at Makaha in the 1970s, my daughters played with her daughter, Jan, at Rell's house. Rell came to our parties, and I always loved being out in the water with her. After Betty and I stopped surfing, and until I returned to Makaha for good in 1990, we didn't spend much time together—we were all heading in different directions.

In 1982, Rell felt a lump in her breast while toweling off during a surfing tour. She was thirty-two, in great physical shape, and at the height of her surfing powers as the top-ranked female longboarder. She fought breast cancer hard. Toward the end of her fourteen-year battle, she discovered a film (made, coincidentally, by my classmate and future husband Bob Liljestrand) about a summer kayaking trip once taken by canoe paddler Audrey Sutherland. The mother of renowned surfer Jock Sutherland, Audrey described her journey along the east side of Molokai in a book, *Paddling My Own Canoe*.

Rell decided to put together a group to follow Audrey's trip. Her sisters and several friends, including me, bought canoes and camping equipment and shipped our gear to Molokai. A high school classmate of Rell's, Glen Davis, escorted us down the rugged coast. Ever since I had spent that summer at Kalaupapa, I had been curious about this coast, with its remote shoreline, its shark-infested blue-black water, its steep cliffs, and its valleys that had welcomed the first Polynesians to land from the Marquesas Islands. For me, it was an uncomfortable journey, sleeping on rocks with minimal supplies, but Rell loved it.

Following the trip, I stopped by her house on my way home from work at the high school. That fall, I could see she was losing strength, and contusions were surfacing in multiple places on her body. But Rell was always upbeat, preferring to recount recent events than to dwell on her health.

In early December 1997, she came to say goodbye. Rell arrived in the afternoon and sat on the rattan couch next to Betty in her antique

Windsor wooden chair. They compared notes on surfing. Rell spoke of her first encounter with Betty and how much she admired the life the older surfer had carved out for herself. Betty told Rell how much she admired her surfing and her work promoting the Makaha Menehune Surf Meet.

"Betty, you and your friends were the first generation of Makaha women surfers," Rell said. "You took up a sport for fun and for freedom."

"And for a more satisfying life," Betty interjected.

"You and Ethel opened up the sport for us."

Of course, Betty realized how professional surfers like Rell were expanding the possibilities for women surfers further than she and Ethel Kukea might ever have imagined. "I wish I could have started surfing at a younger age, like you," she said.

On January 2, 1998, at forty-seven, Rell lost her battle with cancer. Betty, Gloria, and I left the house together, walked for fifteen quiet and sad minutes down the beach, and joined thousands of others for Rell's memorial service. Her family gathered in one canoe with Dave Parmenter, her husband, who held a large etched-glass ball containing her ashes. The waves were running high—a good six to eight feet. Brian Keaulana, Buffalo and Momi's son, gave Rell one last, spectacular ride, paddling the canoe out to the lineup at her favorite break. He caught a big wave and came sliding in toward shore with the wave breaking on the left. Disaster loomed—it looked as though the canoe was going to flip. The crowd on the beach cheered and clapped. Just before the shore-break picked up, Brian turned the canoe back out to the right, over the lip of the wave, and the crew paddled back out to the first blowhole, where Rell's ashes were scattered. Dozens of other canoes joined them, splashing their paddles, throwing flowers, and jumping into the water for one final swim with Rell.

The Queen of Makaha had asked that her funeral mourners not speak of her passing on to a better place. "There's no better place than Makaha," she said. "This is heaven on Earth."

CHAPTER 14

LAST YEARS AT MAKAHA (1990–2011)

I had left Hawaii in 1962 to marry Ron Durand. For most of my teenage years, my male friends had been older, and I was ill prepared for a marriage with a boy my age. We were both too young for it, and I soon learned that we lacked common values and interests. I hated San Jose and the suburban life, and living in an inland Northern California town during the winter made me miserable. Eventually, Ron and I moved to Santa Barbara, near the ocean, but the marriage failed after seven years, leaving us defeated but graced with two wonderful daughters, Marcie and Rennie and eventually six grandchildren.

While living in California, I dreamed of getting my daughters through school and returning to Makaha. After Marcie and Rennie started college, I decided it would be a good idea to get myself a college degree. I started with an associate's degree in manufacturing management and years later ended with a post-master's degree and a secondary teaching degree. It was a long haul for me as a reentry student. By 1990, my daughters were on their own and I had my degrees. I headed back home to Makaha.

Gloria had lived in the back studio on Mother's property for twelve years and was settled in. Besides holding various jobs in Honolulu, she and my mother co-parented Shelley, Gloria's daughter, and Sean, her son. Shelley herself had two children (Bijou and Tony) but was unable to parent them, so Gloria and Betty raised them, too. Betty helped to pay for them to attend private schools in Honolulu.

There were no living quarters for me. My mother, without any hesitation, decided to transform half of the second garage she and Charlie had built adjacent to the house. She called in a carpenter and had one side walled off, leaving space for her car. She put in sliding glass doors and windows. After some finishing work, I had a place to live—the second studio on the property. Later, she added a bathroom and kitchen. The following year, I tacked on two patios and a sleeping porch, and we converted the former garage into a comfortable living space that became my domain.

In November 2005, Rennie came to Makaha for a Thanksgiving vacation with three of her four children, ages five, eight, and eleven. On the third day of her visit, she confided to me that she did not want to go back home to Southern California. She had married Mr. Wrong, a narcissist from La Jolla who had left her for another woman with four children to support. Her story was, of course, familiar to both my mother and me. We welcomed them. Rennie got a teaching job at the local elementary school, and she and her kids lived with us for almost four years. During this time, Rennie spent quality time with her tutu (Hawaiian for "grandmother"). She sorted out her life and left Makaha stronger and happier, thanks to my mother's patience, guidance, influence, and love.

"One of the last conversations we had face-to-face stays with me always," Rennie remembers. "I had decided to move to North Carolina, and I was questioning my decision. 'What if I'm making a mistake?' I asked Tutu. 'Oh, Rennie,' she said, 'it is the same here every day. You go see those wild horses and experience life.' 'But what if I'm making a mistake?' I repeated. She replied, 'That's the fun in life, Rennie. When you make a mistake, the real fun is getting yourself out of it.'"

I had moved back to Makaha shortly after Charlie died. I'm sure that I was seeking to reignite the connection I had as a teenage surfer with a cool surfer mom. But now the tables had turned: I was the one who was busy doing and working. I taught at Wai'anae High School for twelve years, before returning to the clothing business. Finally, once again, I was dyeing textiles and creating fashions. By this time, my mother was approaching her nineties. I was preoccupied with my work and delayed inquiring about her life, as I had hoped to do. It was also hard to ask her certain questions, when her problems were always fastened in her psychological strongbox.

But my failure to probe was partly my own fault. I would try to converse while working, but I was always on some kind of a deadline and it was hard to take breaks until the job was completed. Much of my work was sun-printing sarongs and scarfs on four-by-eight-foot plywood tables on the ocean-side lawn. Nature was my inspiration, but it was also my taskmaster. I had to work while the sun was high and before the wind came up. I checked on Betty between jobs, circling over to her porch or passing through the house for a brief check-in. While we chatted, I would keep moving, circling back to hear the last words of her sentence. She would often say, "Slow down; you move too fast." I was on a mission.

While her attitude was as sprightly as ever, throughout this period my mother had to confront her own physical decline. In June 1990, two weeks after I had arrived home, Mother had been diagnosed with macular degeneration, for which there were fewer treatments then. I was saddened and wondered how such a project-driven woman could live without her eyesight. To my way of thinking, going blind seemed like the worst thing that could possibly happen to her. Luckily, it was a slow process over the next years and she never complained. In fact, Betty said she would rather be blind than lose her hearing, as her brother Herbert had. She preferred to be able to listen to music and converse with people. True to her nature, she never let any tragedy get in the way of her joy at being alive. I could tell she was always thankful to wake up and have another day listening to the sounds of the ocean.

Waves breaking on rocks
They have a certain rhythm
Beautiful to hear

—Betty, 2008

Betty still loved driving her black Caddy around town and into Honolulu, but as the macular degeneration progressed, her eyesight became a serious impairment. The doctors finally laid down the law— no more driving. Being a daredevil, she snuck in one last, four-mile trip to Wai'anae. We didn't know about this jaunt until afterward, when she confessed how scared she had been driving back home when she could barely see the road.

Even as her eyesight was failing, Betty's inner vision was clear. She spoke about saving the Makaha property for my sister and me. My mother was generous: We all lived there rent-free, as she considered it a family commune. After she was gone, she wanted it to be a place for her daughters to live, or an asset we could sell, before going our own ways.

> As memory fades
> Use your imagination
> Try for some color
>
> —Betty, 2010

When one door closed for Betty, she opened another. In 1992, at eighty-six, she purchased a potter's wheel, set it up just outside the kitchen door, and began sculpting bowls and cups. She made ocean-themed pottery with the colors of the sea and the sand. Betty attended a local pottery group, where she improved her skills and socialized. The group met twice a week at the Wai'anae Recreation Center, and those sessions made her day. My sister and I took turns driving her to class and picking her up.

Bunky Bakutis, a master potter, surfer, and friend, was the teacher. A single father, Bunky reflected on Betty as "a woman with characteristics any father would wish upon his daughter: her strength of character, kindness, and willingness to live life to the fullest. She kept challenging herself despite age and disabilities." She was able to make pottery by feel—"seeing" via her sense of touch. Betty's combination of humility and hilarity made her a role model for the class. Bunky said her presence was "a blessing." Another friend, Lyn, helped her with glazes. Betty called this new interest her "creative clay work" and gave most of it away to friends.

Betty creating a bowl at pottery class. Courtesy of
The Honolulu Advertiser, April 18, 2005

The Limelight

In 1996, I received a telephone call from an old friend, the surfer Marge Calhoun. Marge said the entrepreneur Denny Moore was opening a series of surf shops in Hawaii called Malibu Shirts. He planned to sell vintage-inspired T-shirts and surf wear and was looking for surfing memorabilia for the Lewers Street store in Waikiki, which would highlight Makaha history. Denny had already purchased trophies from Marge, Rabbit Kekai, and Ricky Grigg. Would we want to sell Betty's silver cup from Lima, her Makaha 1956 second-place surfing trophy, and my first-place trophy from Makaha in 1957.

My mother and I were surprised and began a long discussion on what to do with our trophies, which—aside from her silver cup in the living room—were hiding out in various closets. We hated to part with them, but we liked the idea of having them on display in the Waikiki shop, where many might learn about Makaha surf history. In the deal, Denny crowned us Malibu Shirts Legends.

Malibu Shirts store grand opening, 2007. From left: Rabbit Kekai,
Clarence Maki, Betty, Vicky, Ricky Grigg, and Peter Cole

Denny made T-shirts with a picture of each of the Legends on the
front. A four-by-five-inch booklet was attached to each shirt, with a picture on the cover and a description of the Legend's life. It gave customers
who purchased the shirts a sense of the featured surfer. (My mother used
some of her money to print up the first copies of a book of haiku poems.)

In 2007, when the redeveloped area of Lewers Street opened, we Legends were invited to attend the ceremony. The street was closed off for the
celebration, which started with a Hawaiian blessing, followed by Hawaiian food, music, and a book signing. My mother was then ninety-four
years old. To make our trip from Makaha easier, we were given a room
at a hotel around the corner, on Saratoga Road. It was a royal getaway.

In 2008, Jane Schmauss, a curator of the California Surf Museum
in Oceanside, California, heard about Betty, her surfing, and her life. Jane
was working on a museum exhibit titled *WOW: Women on Waves—A
History of Women in Surfing*. She visited us in Makaha, and we clicked.
Betty was featured as a pioneer in the exhibit, which included a decade-
by-decade description of the evolution of women's surfing. The exhibit

ran from March 2010 to February 2011. Betty was pictured on a Makaha wave, on the top of a bookmark, as "the Pioneering Surfer," with pictures of Jericho Poppler and Bethany Hamilton below. The exhibit featured sketches of surfers dating back to precontact days in Hawaii and highlighted the growth of surfing as a woman's sport. A collection of women's surfboards included Bethany Hamilton's board, with a chunk torn out from an infamous shark bite. The display also traced the evolution of beach fashions over the years: wool swim dresses in the 1920s, bikinis in the 1960s, and the introduction of board shorts.

Only Seek the Good

Over time, Betty's social group shrank into a smaller group that gathered just for cocktails and conversation. The interactions could get tedious, but sometimes they became heated, especially leading up to the 2008 presidential election, when my mother and I were the only Obama partisans on the porch. Betty admired Barack's intellect. She was thrilled to have shared her first book of haiku with him via his grandmother, who lived next door to my sister's best friend in Honolulu. Barack, in turn, sent her a personally autographed copy of *Dreams of My Father*. Even if we avoided politics at social gatherings, just before the elections, my mother and I attended an evening caucus at the Wai'anae library to cast our votes for Barack. Standing was by now extremely difficult for her, but she wouldn't tolerate the thought of not participating in this ritual of democracy, especially when Barack Obama was on the ballot.

Visitors continued to come by to check on Betty and her projects. Occasionally I complained and wondered why she put up with some of them staying so long. But she still saw the best in every human being and always focused on visitors' good qualities. Later, in the box, I found a poem that Betty had typed up as a young woman. It was titled "Philosophy" and expressed Betty's creed:

> *Now if you'll only seek the good*
> *In the average sort of man,*
> *You'll be quite pleased with your results*

From this simple little plan.
For when you add with kindly thought
Some word in goodly grace,
A spark of love glows in your heart,
And a smile steals o'er his face.

Betty and Charlie had constructed a large lanai right off the kitchen and living room. This covered area overlooked the front yard, the coconut trees, the beach, and the ocean. It was comfortable and protected from sun and rain. They also built a rectangular teak table, and Betty tiled the top with small blue squares reminiscent of the ocean's colors. It accommodated three people on each side and one at each end. My mother, Gloria, and I—as well as assorted children and guests—usually ate breakfast, lunch, and dinner out there. But Betty spent many additional hours at her designated seat at the head of the table. She listened to the rhythmic sounds of the waves hitting the beach, an almost fleeting, barely audible, but constant murmur, along with the wind, the birds, and the rustle of palm fronds.

Betty treasured aloneness with her thoughts. She enjoyed many happy hours of contemplation on her lanai. She was often entertained by the chirping of geckos and, before she lost her eyesight, by watching cardinals landing and eating the cooked rice she had put out on the front lawn for them.

Speaking of friendships
Everyone should have a bird
It won't deceive you

—Betty 2010

My mother composed many haiku on her porch. When she couldn't see to write the verses, she memorized them until my sister came along to jot down the lines on paper and then type them up.

In her final years, a favorite pastime of Betty's was listening to the weekly *Science Friday* program on the radio. Ever the scientist, she was particularly fascinated by the moon, sky, and ocean, but her interests were broad. She wrote one skeptical haiku about lunar exploration. I chuckle remembering the time she said, "Vicky, something very interesting for the computer is coming out. It is called the cloud."

She also listened to books on tape and *Time* magazine from the Library for the Blind, as well as spiritual tapes and a Sunday-morning radio show featuring New Age thinkers. Betty was not a religious person, although she believed that the institution of the church gave order to society. She rejected dogma and theology. The Golden Rule—do unto others as you would have them do unto you—was enough for her.

"A Little Bit More"

Over Betty's last years, she willed herself to live, and we all worked hard to match her determination. Being in the sun over a lifetime without a hat and/or sunscreen had wreaked havoc on her skin. Several times, she had had small skin cancers removed from her face and legs. She had a heart murmur and took medicine for it, but when she turned ninety-one, in 2001, it became clear that she needed a heart-valve replacement. Because she was in such good physical shape, Dr. Ito, a surgeon and the son of a neighbor who had bought the Sumidas' place, agreed to do the operation. (By the age of ninety, a person is usually thought too old to go through the procedure.) Betty came out with flying colors, having to take only Tylenol for pain. The experience gave her a higher quality of life in her final years.

She had had a knee replacement in her seventies and had a hip patched after a fall when she was ninety-seven. Incredibly, each medical incident seemed only to increase her zest. Betty out-survived most of her friends and siblings. Of course, this saddened her, but she went on to make new friends and had a special rapport with the younger ones.

When a bout of bronchitis led us to take Betty to the emergency room at the Wai'anae Comprehensive Health Clinic in 2007, Dr. Carolyn Annerud, the emergency doctor on duty, cared for her. During conversations, we discovered that Dr. Carolyn also lived in Makaha, in an apartment at the opposite end of the beach—just walking distance away. Betty and Dr. Carolyn bonded immediately. She, too, was a sportswoman, a surfer, and stand-up paddler. Dr. Carolyn was fifty, with the strength of an athlete. Of Swedish descent, she had bobbed blond hair and blue eyes and dressed smartly when not in a bathing suit. Dr. Carolyn was soft-spoken but always had something meaningful to say. Sometimes she brought delicacies to the house for lunch or dinner. And, mysteriously, she often showed up when Betty needed her expertise in a health crisis. My mother laughingly called her "my angel."

When not working shifts at the emergency room, Dr. Carolyn practiced medicine with Doctors Without Borders in New Guinea. She took trips to exotic lands and over the years would share her experiences with Betty, who lived vicariously through them. They became not just the best of friends, but soul mates.

At ninety-seven, Mother decided one Saturday morning that she needed to return to the site of many fond memories, the gorgeous pink Royal Hawaiian Hotel in Waikiki. It was Dr. Carolyn's birthday. Her friend would be celebrating it in Waikiki, and Betty wanted to be there to surprise her.

Neither my sister nor I was at home. Betty confided in Rennie about her plan and asked her granddaughter to help her prepare for the thirty-six-mile trip. Betty's next-door neighbor Ken dropped by to say hello, and she told him what she wanted to do. He, too, was headed for town and said he would be happy to give her a ride. (The hour bus ride would have involved a transfer at a busy area at Ala Moana Center.) Betty picked up her bag, brushed her hair, put on lipstick, and climbed into Ken's car. She arrived at the Royal Hawaiian and was shown to her room, where she sat and waited. Her poor vision prevented her from leaving the room or even using the phone to call room service. Dr. Carolyn surfaced in the late afternoon, and the two celebrated, driving back to Makaha together the next morning.

Around this time, in 2009, my sister found out about an essay contest sponsored by the *Honolulu Star-Advertiser*'s Midweek edition, in conjunction with Governor Linda Lingle's eighth annual Honolulu Women's Leadership Conference. Participants were to write a 250-word essay describing how another woman inspired them to give "a little bit more."

Betty and Dr. Carolyn entered the contest separately, neither knowing that the other had also done so. My mother dictated her essay, and

Gloria typed it up and sent it off. The winner would attend the Honolulu Women's Leadership Conference at the Sheraton Waikiki.

A few weeks later came the news that two essays had won: Betty's and Dr. Carolyn's. Both women were invited to the conference. My sister was traveling, so I took Mother to town. The hotel provided a room so that we could be at the conference first thing in the morning.

My mother's essay began simply: "My name is Betty P. Winstedt. I am in my ninety-seventh year and live at the beach in Makaha." My mother then described how she had met Dr. Carolyn: "In the emergency room, I was treated by Dr. Carolyn Annerud, whom I mistook for an angel, thinking I was on my way to meet Saint Peter."

The essay continued to describe their friendship:

On one of her visits, she found me writing haiku poetry, which she thought was pretty amazing, as I am legally blind. She volunteered to type them, as my writing is so scribbly. As time passed and the haiku poems increased, she said, "We're going to have to do something with these. Why don't you put them in a book?" When I commented that they weren't good enough, she insisted they were, and inspired me to get started. A neighbor who does desktop publishing volunteered to format the haiku poems and photos into book form, and it has become an unanticipated success.

Carolyn told me to keep swimming, get back to pottery, stand up straight, and walk as much as possible. Carolyn, thank you for the encouragement. You have pushed the right button and I love it. You have inspired me to keep on going beyond my ninety-six years.

Carolyn's essay began much more dramatically:

She was fighting for breath. It was 1:00 a.m. and the emergency department was packed. I introduced myself as the emergency physician on duty, did a brief exam, gave orders to the nurse, and moved on to the next patient.

By 4:00 a.m. she was feeling better and we had a chance to talk. At ninety-one, this tall, elegant woman still had the firm muscle tone of an athlete—she'd surfed until she was sixty and still swam daily.

Carolyn continued by describing how the two became unlikely "soul mates." Betty grounded her, she said, as the two shared "secrets and sadnesses."

Betty was my virtual "wing-woman" when I finished the solo stand-up paddleboard race across the Molokai Channel in July. I think she was more excited—before and afterwards—than I was, if that is possible. Each time I thought I might not make it, I knew that I couldn't quit, because of Betty.

Betty is now ninety-seven. When her eyesight failed, she took up pottery because she could feel and work the clay. Each time I eat from one of her beautiful bowls, I feel her strength. When sitting and working at the pottery wheel hurt her back, she began writing haiku, eventually publishing a book of her work.

Betty is a constant reminder that strength and beauty come from within, that each day is a gift that we give to ourselves, and that a positive life is a personal choice.

The essays inspired hundreds of women in the audience. Betty pre-sold early copies of her first haiku book. She basked in the limelight.

A few weeks later, an editor from the *Honolulu Advertiser* called to say that the paper had heard about an inspirational woman who lived at Makaha and wanted to send out a writer and photographer to do a story. Gwen Kawela's article appeared on the front page of the newspaper's "Living" section and began:

Betty Heldreich Winstedt has lived the kind of adventures that could fill the pages of a novel. A pioneer of women's surfing, a jeweler, potter and pilot, her philosophies on life include "try anything exciting" and "it's never too late to learn."

Once an Olympic swimming hopeful, she learned to pilot small planes, took up longboarding at the age of forty, and traveled the world as an international surf competitor, counting legendary Waikiki beach boys among her surfing friends.

A televised interview with Maile Shimabukuro—the Waiʻanae Democratic representative to the Hawaii State Senate—followed the newspaper article. Maile came to the house and sat at the table out on our front porch. Betty summarized her surfing life. She explained why, at age ninety-seven, she started writing haiku. She said, "I live right next to the beach, but I cannot swim in the ocean, surf, walk on the beach, or drive a car anymore. I have to figure out something else to do. There are so many subjects to speak and write about, and I write haiku whenever I see or think of something interesting. Putting thoughts in concise words is a challenge—there are only three lines to tell a story."

Betty's great-granddaughter Maile played the piano in the background while Betty recited some of her favorite haiku, whose subjects ranged from silly to reflective. They described nature and, occasionally, surfing.

Betty swimming with dolphins at Pōkaʻī Bay, 2008

Large whales passing by
On their winter long swim north
Seeking warm water

Angry squawking birds
Ready to attack the cat
Demons from the sky

All sports have their place
Surfing days have passed me by
Time to watch others

Quiet time alone
The spirit whispers to us
The truth is revealed

—Betty, 2007–09

CHAPTER 15

REMINISCENCE

One of Betty's favorite stories involved backing her car out of the garage in Makaha. She noticed a paper had dropped on the ground outside her car window. Without thinking, and without putting the car in park, she put her foot on the brake, opened the car door, and leaned out to pick it up. But she leaned so far out that she fell out of the driver's seat and onto the dirt driveway. The car was in reverse, so Betty had to lie on the ground until she could get herself out of this situation. If she moved or took her foot off the brake, the car would run over her and crash into the workshops. She yelled for someone to come and help. My sister heard her shouts. From the ground, Mother directed Gloria to slip into the front seat from the passenger side and put her foot on the brake. Then she could take her own foot off and stand up to put the car in park. That is exactly what happened. Betty expressed her relief with typical terseness: "That was a close call."

Whether facing cheating husbands or destructive tsunamis, Betty never saw herself as a victim. She was a true stoic, but she also let her zest for life take over. In fact, she thought the fun of life was getting out of scrapes. (This attitude suited her perfectly for surfing Makaha.) She remained courageous and adventurous until her last breath. "I was a child who knew the world to be a wonderful place," she wrote in her autobiography as a young woman. "Bewildering events have followed, but never sorrow." A relentless optimist, Betty believed that adversity is just a door to opportunity.

Jane Schmauss, from the California Surf Museum, met Betty in 2009 and remembers that at ninety-six, Betty was "blessed with keen intelligence." She continued, "Her calmness and confidence pulled me in like a magnet: I wanted to learn from her, listen to her stories, and tap into the source of her strength. Her sharp memory could call upon many lessons from the past, but she lived in the present and thought a great deal about the future. Betty's sense of kindness, quick wit, and ready humor enriched everyone around her."

"Betty inspired me to be a better person by her own high personal ethics and discipline, and encouraged me in my aspirations as an aging waterwoman," wrote Dr. Carolyn Annerud, my mother's last and best-ever friend. "Some people thought we had a special code-talk, but it was more like we were thirteen years old and able to talk about anything and everything—to giggle, and laugh, and cry, and question everything in the universe—whether or not we could answer our own questions. Betty told me she did not believe in God, at least not as a separate person. But she believed there was God and goodness in each of us."

> Life is a journey
> Full of change and surprises
> Ah sweet mystery
>
> —Betty, 2011

In 2011, at ninety-eight, my mother was living what she called a happy and quiet life at Makaha Beach. She sat in her chair on the lanai and listened to the ocean. Her memories were filled with young surfers, the group of people she surfed with, and her most exciting rides. She said she felt lucky to have enjoyed the "early" days in Waikiki, when she was able to know Duke Kahanamoku, Charlie Amalu, and other old-time surfers.

At ninety-six, Betty missed male companionship and occasionally told us she would like to meet a younger man—eighty-six years old would be fine. ("I like handsome men," she mused in one haiku.) She nursed yet another goal, one she'd held for a long time: to live until she was one hundred, or at least make it to her ninety-ninth year, when she figured she would actually have lived a hundred years.

In August 2011, halfway through her ninety-eighth year, Betty mysteriously contracted a blood pathogen and was hospitalized. A stent was inserted in her chest near her heart for antibiotic treatments. After two weeks, she was released from the hospital, but she would need to continue the treatments daily as an outpatient. Logistically, this would be hard to manage from Makaha. My fiancé, Bob Liljestrand, invited her to stay in his family home on Mt. Tantalus in Honolulu. The Liljestrand House is a remarkable example of mid-twentieth-century Hawaiian architecture, and Bob and his siblings were in the process of turning the home into a foundation and museum. They set up the guest room for my mother. From there, she could easily make it to the hospital for treatments.

While Betty was ill, we sat on the lanai of this house and looked out over all of Honolulu—from Diamond Head to Pearl Harbor. Her beloved Wai'anae Coast was out of sight, around the bend at Kapolei, but it was in her mind. We talked about our lives together.

She touched on her greatest challenges: training in freestyle swimming for the Olympics while feeling a constant hunger; working as a capable young hygienist whose patients doubted her abilities; coping with a moody and philandering husband over twenty-two years; watching her second husband battle Parkinson's disease; losing Charlie; losing her own vision and freedom of movement.

But, true to form, in those days at the Liljestrand House, Betty didn't dwell on hardship. She reflected on the most joyous times, when she had worked on various projects: carving wax models for the jewelry business; creating menehune charms in Honolulu; building a house at Makaha; setting up a lab; helping Charlie finish his fishing boat and heading out to sea with him. And, of course, there was surfing.

I couldn't help but reflect on how surfing was a gift my mother and I gave to each other. Of course, there was the sheer athleticism, the physical and psychological strength it fostered in both of us. And there was the camaraderie, the deep connection to nature, the bond with each other, the fun of meeting the challenge of every new wave—and the confidence to look for continual challenges that enriched our lives. But it was even more than that. When I was twelve and returned home from Hawaii and told her I did not want to live in Chino, my mother heard the unhappiness in my voice, and, more important, she *listened* to it. She decided to visit Hawaii to see what had moved me.

After one summer vacation, Betty, too, fell in love with the islands, and she uprooted her own life in Chino. Soon enough, she learned to surf; ended an unhappy marriage; built a house on one of the most beautiful beaches in the world; started a new career; married a fisherman; and established a sanctuary for herself, her family, and her friends.

After one week, Betty decided she had to get back to Makaha. She was tired of being away from home, and she missed the sound of the waves. On her last morning on Mt. Tantalus, we packed up her belongings and then stopped at the St. Francis outpatient hospital for a final treatment. Curiously, just before it, she held my eyes with hers and said, "I feel that I am going, going up. I am not going down." Knowing I would struggle to understand, she added, "Vicky, you have to accept this." I tried to stay calm.

Dr. Carolyn dropped by the outpatient room at the hospital, bringing a Jamba Juice mango smoothie and a carrot-zucchini muffin. My mother happily quaffed her smoothie and nibbled at the muffin. During the infusion, they visited about many things: her privileged upbringing, losing the house, the good times they had together, their love of the water, President Obama, the black-white situation in America, and how happy she would be to get home to her genius loci, Makaha.

As the nurse, Delia, was removing the IV, she slipped away.

> White cloud over grey
> Sailing high above the storm
> Boldly like courage
>
> —Betty, 2010

In the many days and nights that followed, one of the stories she had told me kept playing out as a vision in my head. It was in the summer of 1959, at Keawaʻula—in recent years known by surfers as Yokohama. The Hawaiian name literally means "Red Harbor" and refers to the numerous cuttlefish that swim in the bay. In ancient Hawaii, it was believed that spirits of the newly dead came here; if ʻaumakua (personal gods) thought a person wasn't ready to die, they would turn the spirit back to reenter the body. Later, the Oahu Railroad train stopped here to let off Japanese fisherman, many of whom were from Yokohama, Japan, and the bay acquired its modern name.

Yokohama is located ten miles from Makaha, down an uninhabited two-lane road—just before the road ends at Kaʻena Point. It is an unpeopled and desolate spot on Oahu, and one of the most splendid. The beach, with its blue-green crystalline water and wide swath of white sand, faces directly west and is backed by the rugged, plunging Waiʻanae mountains, emerald-green in winter and spring, dry brown in late summer and fall. Ocean swells come in directly from the sea, hit the shallow shore, studded with jagged coral heads, and form a peak. Thick, powerful waves unfurl over the rocky bottom. It is a scary and dangerous place to surf.

Over the years, Betty developed respect for this break and longed to surf there. "I decided to put my fear on the back burner, test my skill, my luck, and surf Yokohama," Betty told me, remembering that summer of 1959. "I could see from the house that the south swell was up and pumping. After driving out to the beach and taking my board off the car, I sat and watched for a while to get a sense of the waves. I paddled out to the lineup and sat up on my board, feeling a sense of thrill but at the same time intimidation. I knew the danger that lurked. I waited for what I thought would be the perfect wave. It came. I took a deep breath, paddled a few strokes, stood up, and headed down the steep, six-foot face. Soon I found myself crouched inside a tubing corridor of water. This was like nothing I had experienced before; I felt a sense of awe. In the semidarkness, I could see just a glimmer of light at the far end. The world seemed to slow down. Even the thundering wave went silent. Peter Cole had once described such a ride as surrealistic, almost mystical. It was. I experienced a supernatural, intense bliss—rapture, really. I shot out to the other end, still standing. For an instant, the whole world was silent."

The tree is ancient.
One strong wind laid it to rest.
It is still alive.

—Betty, 2011

APPENDIX

ENGLAND TO SALT LAKE CITY

(1850–1929)

Betty's ancestors were ardent adventurers who made indelible contributions to Utah's early pioneer history. She had hardworking and talented great-grandfathers on her father's side of the family: Richard Bishop Margetts and Herbert Earl Pembroke, both early residents of Salt Lake City.

Great-grandfather James Earl Pembroke and his wife, Sarah Day, immigrated to the Salt Lake Valley in 1868. Economic times were difficult in Bedford, England, where they belonged to the English mission of the Mormon Church. In 1866, Brigham Young recruited church people with the promise of land and a better life in Utah. James Earl Pembroke was seventy-two years old when he left England, accompanied by fifty-three-year-old Sara and three teenage children: Phoebe Jane, eighteen; Herbert Earl, fifteen; and Mary Ann, twelve.

The Pembrokes traveled on the *American Congress* ship to New York, from May 23 to July 5, 1866, arriving, symbolically, the day after Independence Day.

In December 1866, the family was advised to wait until battles between Montana plains Indians Crazy Horse and Red Cloud and the US Cavalry settled down before they headed to Salt Lake. James worked at his "line of art in the job of printing" in New York until it was safe to head west.

In 1868, the family took the train to from New York to Laramie, Wyoming (as far west as the train traveled). From Wyoming, they boarded a wagon train for the five-week, rough trek to Salt Lake City. There were sixty-six families, all Mormons, on thirty-three wagons, two families to each wagon. The women and children rode while the men and boys walked behind or alongside. At night, the wagons formed a circle and the pioneers built a fire, cooked dinner, mended clothes, prayed, and sang hymns. Pioneer diaries of the wagon train trip recount a treacherous and rugged journey. The pioneer settlers made their way across rivers without bridges, untraveled terrain, and Indian territory. They faced off against occasional bandits who were after their livestock and money. An older woman and two young children died along the way, and there were many hardships.

Betty's great-grandfather Richard Bishop Margetts also came to the Salt Lake Valley from England as an early Mormon convert. He and his family members sailed aboard the *Argo* from Liverpool to New Orleans from January 10, 1850, to March 11, 1850. At the foot of the Mississippi River, they then boarded a smaller ship to go upriver to the city of Saint Louis. After several months, Richard Margetts became sick and vowed to die, rather than spend another steamy summer there. He built his own wagon for the six-month trip across the plains to Salt Lake City. Richard Margetts chronicled his ocean voyage but did not keep a journal for the wagon trip.

Edward Tullidge, author of *The History of Salt Lake*, describes Richard Margetts as follows: "Not in any sense an orthodox religious man. He was a perfectly liberal Mormon, but believed in a grander spirit of humanitarianism rather than the strife of the present day makes possible. He liked to dream of the day to come when all mankind would be united in a universal brotherhood." This was an unusual outlook for this period in Mormon Salt Lake City.

As a young man in England, Richard had received blacksmith training from his father, and when he first lived in Salt Lake, he worked at this trade. During this time, he tried to get a pair of boots made by a man who owned a tanning business, in trade for beef. The boot maker refused, so Richard built his own tannery and tanned hides until it was no longer economically feasible. He also built and started the first brewery in the Salt Lake Valley, the Utah Brewery. In *Beer in the Beehive: A History of Brewing in Utah*, Del Vance writes, "The early pioneers lived by a different set of rules than today. They drank beer and whiskey but believed in moderation rather than total abstinence. Like the Puritans before them, they didn't consider beer to be liquor." The early Mormons produced a whiskey called Valley Tan. "By 1870, three-fourths of Utah's revenue came from the sale of alcoholic beverages," Vance adds.

Richard Margetts, one of the earliest expert iron workers, was a progressive, public-spirited citizen, highly esteemed, and an active member of the community. A nature lover, he imported the first sparrows, supposedly singing sparrows, but they didn't sing, were very messy, and ended up being the nemesis of Salt Lake City. He was also the first to plant celery. He established coal lands and invented an oven for processing coal. He was an ardent believer in the principle of home manufacture and entrepreneurship.

Richard planned and made the first metal cane mill used for processing sugar beets in the Utah Territory. During these years, sugar beets were an important source of income, and also needed to be processed into molasses. Richard's plant was made mostly of old wagon tires. He was also involved in silver mining and believed Utah's iron and coal deposits were the key to his prosperity. Unfortunately, he died at fifty-eight before he could live this dream.

The Next Generations

Herbert Earl Pembroke, Betty's grandfather, was eighteen when he arrived in Salt Lake City with his parents, James Earl and Sarah Day Pembroke. He joined his father's trade in the printing business. He first worked as a journeyman printer for the *Salt Lake Tribune*. After a time, he wanted to learn more about the printing business and left to work for H.S. Crocker & Co., a large printing company with offices in Sacramento and San Francisco. He spent three years there, before returning to Salt Lake City and marrying Sarah Jane Margetts.

Sarah was the daughter of Richard Bishop Margetts. After a few months in Salt Lake, the couple returned to San Francisco, where Herbert Earl worked for another four years for Crocker & Co.

According to Tullidge in *The History of Salt Lake*, Herbert had remarkable artistic skills and was the best printer in the city. He saw a niche for a new retail venture and believed it was time to start his own business. He and his brother Adrian, opened a book, stationery, and news store called the Pembroke Stationery Company. Over the years, it became a well-known landmark in Salt Lake City.

By the time Herbert Earl Pembroke died, his wife, Sarah (my mother's paternal grandmother), had already given up on Mormonism. Upon his death, the church promised to reunite husband and wife in heaven after their deaths—for a fee. "No, thank you," she said. "I have had quite enough of this man right here on Earth!"

Betty's parents, Earl and Elizabeth Pembroke, were freethinkers and abandoned the Mormon Church in 1910. As a child, Earl had been forced to give up his bed to traveling Mormon missionaries, and he despised their hypocrisy, violent faith, and underhanded dealings with Indians or anyone else who did not go along with Mormon dogma. Earl and Elizabeth lived not just outside Mormon convention but outside convention, period. Earl never fully recovered from his financial loss in Salt Lake. The business reversals caused him to seek solace in alcohol. In their later years, Earl and Elizabeth lived separately, though they never divorced.

A NOTE ON HAWAIIAN

LANGUAGE AND STYLE

During much of the period this book covers, and especially in the 1950s and '60s, Hawaiian language ('ōlelo Hawai'i) was on the wane, and many words were commonly mispronounced and misunderstood. Some were also appropriated by mass culture—and surfing culture—and acquired slightly different casts. In the 1970s and '80s, a movement began to better appreciate meaning and nuance in the Hawaiian language and to use spelling conventions that would underscore traditional meaning and pronunciation.

In an acknowledgment of the shifting linguistic tides, we have for the most part used the spellings and markings suggested by Hawaiian language experts and dictionaries. (For example, we retain the diacritical marks in "ho'omalimali" and "'opihi"). We do not italicize these words, as people in the islands do not view them as foreign words.

Individual place names are critically important in Hawaiian language, in which a love of myriad locations and celebration of their legacies is deeply encoded. Their constituent parts often have particular meaning (ka'ena, for example, the name of Oahu's westernmost point, literally means "the heat"; wai mea, which is the root of the storied river, valley, and surfing bay, means "reddish water"). So we have retained diacritical marks and spellings to honor these important traces of meaning in place names, as in Keawa'ula and Wai'anae.

However, if Hawaiians in earlier decades didn't use diacritical marks, we've tried to retain their preferences, as in Earl Akana's Hale Auau. In a few examples, we retain the spellings used by mass culture and, in particular, surf culture. Pop culture has planted "Waikiki," "Makaha," and "Pokai" in our minds, and this is how surfers refer to them, even if scholars would spell these spots "Waikīkī," "Mākaha," and "Pōka'ī"—and pronounce them accordingly.

Similarly, surfers and local residents often use "Westside" to refer to the coastal areas that lie to the west of the Wai'anae Range. In earlier times, Hawaiians did not use cardinal points and tended to use specific place names or words, like "lalo" and "kona," that referred to the side of an island facing away from the prevailing winds, or trade winds; this side is sheltered from much rain by hills and mountains. These Hawaiian terms might be translated as "leeward," and indeed, in more modern times, the western part of the island is also known as the leeward side, although that term also encompasses 'Ewa, Kalaeloa, and even the edge of Pearl Harbor. We have favored the term Betty and her friends used, "Westside," but have also used "Wai'anae Coast" and "leeward side" for variety.

When words have been anglicized and brought into the English lexicon, we use the common English spelling and the English plural form ("leis," "luaus," "muumuu"). For the name of the state, we use Hawaii, and for the names of the major inhabited islands, we use Hawaii, Kauai, Maui, Molokai, Niihau, and Oahu. Again, this is not out of a cavalier disrespect for 'ōlelo Hawai'i, but rather out of a desire to avoid placing speed bumps in the path of the reader.

ENDNOTES

Chapter 1. First Wave (1954)

Chapter 2. Pioneer Origins (1913-29)

Tullidge, Edward W. *The History of Salt Lake City and its Founders: 1829-1894.* Salt Lake City: Edward W. Tullidge Publisher, 2009.

"Earl R. Pembroke, 69, Dies after Long Mine Career." *The Salt Lake Herald*, April 27, 1948.

Research Center of the Utah State Archives and Utah State History. "Rosebank Cottage." *Salt Lake Herald*, April 25, 1886.

Research Center of the Utah State Archives and Utah State Historic Society. City Directory, Salt Lake County Probate Case Files on Microfilm , Salt Lake City Archives, 1886-1934.

Haglund, Kenneth T. & Notarianni, Philip F. *The Avenues of Salt Lake City*. Utah: Utah State Historic Society, 1980.

Haglund, Kenneth T. & Notarianni, Philip F. *The Avenues of Salt Lake City*. Revised and updated by Cevan J. LeSieur - Second edition, Utah: University of Utah Press and the Utah State Historic Society, 2012.

Lester, Margaret D. *Brigham Street*. Utah: Utah State Historical Society, 1979.

"Betty Pembroke Leads St. Mary's Athletic Girls." *Salt Lake Telegram*, October 17, 1929.

Chapter 3. California Dreaming (1929-36)

"Herman Smith Annexes Swim." *Los Angeles Times*, August 19,1935.

The Games of The Xth Olympiad, Los Angeles, California, 1932. Official Report (The American Olympic Committee Report). Los Angeles, California, 1932.

Young, Betty Lou. *Mercury*. Los Angeles: The Los Angeles Athletic Club, Vol. 107; Issue 1, 1979.

Young, Betty Lou. *Our First Century*. Los Angeles: Olympic Club Press, 1979.

Garbutt, Frank A. "The Story of The Los Angeles Athletic Club as told to Its Membership."

"Wounds Confine Glider Aviatrix." *Los Angeles Times*, June 30, 1936.

Chapter 4. Lost Wax and White Gold (1937-51)

Megowan, Maureen. "History of Rancho Palos Verdes." Megowan Realty Group. www.maureenmegowan.com/Pages/history-of-rancho-palos-verdes. Aspv, 1-27.

Megowan, Maureen (real-estate broker) in discussion with the author, October 2017.

Pinkham, Daniel (gatehouse owner) in discussion with the author, October, 2017.

Tapper, Joan. "Santa Catalina." *Islands Magazine*, pg. 55-56, June 2006.

Maxwell, Pat, Rhein, Bob, & Roberts, Jerry. *Catalina A to Z: A Glossary Guide to California's Island Jewel*. Charleston, South Carolina: The History Press, 2014.

"California and the Second World War: The Attacks on the SS Baabara Olson and the SS Absaroka." California Military Department. http://www.militarymuseum.org/Olson.html.

"Lieutenant Faces 3 Years at Labor." *Medford Times*, June 9, 1944.

"Captain William Banning, Son of Wilmington Founder, Dies." *Wilmington Daily Press Journal*, January 28, 1946.

Chapter 5. Hawaii Calls (1954-55)

Law, Anwei Skinsnes. *Kalaupapa, A Collective Memory*. Honolulu: University of Hawai'i Press, 2012.

Tayman, John. *The Colony: the Harrowing True Story of the Exciles of Molokai*. New York City: Scribner, 2007.

"Kalaupapa's Vanishing Faces." *Honolulu Star-Bulletin*, March 30, 2003.

"Kalaupapa." *National Historic Park*.

Chapter 6. The Gold Coast (1954-55)

Puku'i, Mary Kawena & Curtis, Caroline. *Tales of the Menehune*. Honolulu, Hawai'i: Kamehameha Schools Press, 1960.

"Who Was Dad Center." Outrigger Canoe Club. 2019. www.outriggercanoeclubsports.com/canoe-racing/dad-center-race/who-was-george-dad-center/.

Park, Sarah. "Center of the Beach." *Star-Bulletin*, January 16, 1954.

McQueen, Red. "Aloha Dad! God Bless You!" *The Honolulu Advertiser*, September 13, 1962.

"Island Aquatics Leader, 'Dad' Center, Dies at 75." *Star-Bulletin*, September 13, 1962.

Davis, David. *Waterman-The Life and Times of Duke Kahanamoku*. Nebraska: University of Nebraska Press, 2015.

Clark, John R. K. *Hawaiian Surfing/Traditions From The Past*, Honolulu: University of Hawai'i Press, 2011.

Schmitt, Robert C. *Historical Statistics of Hawaii*, Honolulu: The University of Hawai'i Press, 1977.

Honolulu Visitors Bureau in discussion with the author, 2016.

Chapman, William R. *The Story of Hawaii's Volcano House(s)-1844 to the Present*. Hawaii: Hawaii National Park Service, 2016.

Chapter 7. The Westside Story (1956)

Pukui, Mary Kawena, & Elbert, Samuel H. *Hawaiian Dictionary*. Honolulu: University of Hawai'i Press, 1957.

Coleman, Stuart Holmes. *Fierce Heart: The Story of Makaha and the Soul of Hawaiian Surfing*. New York City: St. Martin's Press, 2009.

Lancaster, "John. Exploring the Hidden Culture in Hawai'i." *National Geographic Magazine*, pg. 58-75, 2015.

Smith, Joel & Croci, Ron. *The Illustrated Atlas of Surfing History-Wave Riding from Antiquity to Gidget*. Waipahu, Hawai'i: Island Heritage Publishing, 2016.

Borte, Jason. "Makaha." Surfline, www.surfline.com/surfing-a-to-z-/makaha-history_856/.

Pukui, Mary Kawena, Elbert, Samuel H., & Mookine, Esther T. *Place Names of Hawai'i*. Honolulu: The University of Hawai'i Press, 1976.

Krauss, Bob, McGrath Jr., Edward J. & Brewer, Kenneth M. *Historic Waianae-A Place of Kings*. Norfolk Island, Australia: An Island Heritage Limited, 1973.

Finney, Ben. *The Development and Diffusion of Modern Surfing*, University of Hawai'i, Vol. 69, 314-331, 1960.

Finney, Ben & Houston, James D. *Surfing-The Sport of Hawaiian Kings*. Clarendon, Vermont: Tuttle Publishing, 1966.

Finney, Ben & Houston, James D. *Surfing-A History of the Ancient Sport*. San Francisco: Pomegranate Art books, 1996.

Stevenson, Larry. "Big-wave Surfing Pioneer, Buzzy Trent." *Surf Guide Magazine*, Vol. 1, 1963.

Duane, Daniel. "Taking the Waves." *The New York Times Magazine*, February 10, 2019.

Warshaw, Matt. *The History of Surfing*. San Francisco: San Francisco Chronicle Books, 2010.

Kila, Glen (Director of Marae Ha'a Koa Waianae Cultural Center) in discussion with the author, March 2019.

Chapter 8. Wave Riding Goes Competitive (1957-59)

"Hawaii Surfers to Vie in Peru." *The Honolulu Advertiser*, January 15, 1957.

"Surfing Champion Back from Peru." *The Honolulu Advertiser*, April 15, 1957.

"Public Asked to Help Pay Cost of Surfers' Trip to Peru." *Star-Bulletin*, February 7, 1957.

"Five set for Peru Surfing Meet." *The Honolulu Advertiser*, February 13, 1957

"Hawaii Surf Campion Visiting in Pomona." *The Progress Bulletin*, April 2, 1957.

"They Ride the Wild Waves." *Saturday Evening Post Magazine*, June 14, 1958.

"Makaha Surf Improves: Vicki Heldreich Wins." The Honolulu Advertiser, November 25, 1957.

Chapter 9. New Horizons (1959-60)

Chapter 10. A Sourjourn to South America (1960)

"Campeonato Annual de Tabla Hawaiana se iniciará el Sábado en Kon Tiki." *LaChronica,* February 18, 1960.

Chapter 11. Life After Lima (1961-63)

"Admiral's Son Killed-Huge Seas, Surfboards Flying Everywhere." *The HonoluluAdvertiser*, November 12, 1959.

Chapter 12: Becoming a Fisherwoman (1963-89)

Carter, Bruce. "Marlin Spree - 6 in 26 Hours." *The Honolulu Advertiser,* December 5, 1967.

Gibson, Gordon & Renison, Carol. *Bull of The Woods-The Gordon Gibson Story*, Vancouver: Douglas & McIntyre, 1980.

Chapter 13. Changing Tides (1990)

Zallberg, Sandford. "A Paradise With Problems." *Star-Bulletin*, June 24, 1979.

"Native Hawaiian Program 9 Title VIII Native A Region IX Program." *Alu Like Inc.,* 1977.

"Caner Kills Rell Sunn, Surf Legend." *Star-Bulletin,* January 3, 1998.

"Rell Kapolioka'ehukai Sunn." *The Honolulu Advertiser,* February 8, 1998.

Sunn, Rell, *Heart of the Sea,* produced by Charlotte Lagarde & Lisa Denker (2003; Honolulu: PBS Hawai'i, Film.

Sodetani, Naomi. "Heart of the Sea." *Honolulu Magazine,* 45-47, May 2003.

"Everyone Could Count on 'Rella Propella' to Whip up Some Fun." *The Honolulu Advertiser,* January 5, 1998.

Chapter 14. Last Years in Makaha (1990-11)

Kekaula, Gwen. "A Legend Young at Heart." *The Honolulu Advertiser,* April 18, 2005,

ACKNOWLEDGMENTS

I am deeply indebted to many friends and relatives for helping me bring to life the story of my unusual mother. Without you, I could never even have started. Many thanks to my surfing buddy, old friend, and surf photographer Tom Keck for planting the seeds for this project in 2001, when he suggested I write an article about Betty for *The Surfer's Journal*. Tom came to Makaha and took a series of pictures of my mother with her pottery. Years passed before I came to grips with the idea that this was a project I needed to tackle.

Thanks to Dr. Edith Frampton, who encouraged me and helped me see that it was necessary to tell Betty's story, and the larger surfing story, from my own vantage point.

Thanks to The Utah State Historical Society and Laurie Bryant for her research on Rose Bank Cottage as well as to the many people who are characters in the surfing story and offered help, whether a foreword or a fact-check: Carolyn Annerud, Bunky Bakutis, Dr. Jim Blattau, Marge Calhoun, Peter Cole, John Elwell, Fred Hemmings, Jimmy Heumann, Sheila Fletcher Kriemelman, Jan Lee, Dr. Roland Mauer, Marion Lyman-Mersereau, Joe Quigg, Jane Schmauss, Sooriyakumar, Barbara Sumida, and Carol Wilcox. Others, many writers themselves, have helped me to understand the world of books and publishing: John Clark, Piper Cochran, Stuart Coleman, David Davis, Muffie Wall Dominick, Denby Fawcett, Nadine Ferraro, Heather Hudson, Linde Keil, Matt Lutrell,

David Levy, and Ian Lind. I have a great deal of appreciation to Michelle Au for her untiring technical assistance with scanning and dealing with the computer. Also, thanks to Katherine Strong for her input and help. Providing much-needed historical context were Shirley Ito at LA 84 Foundation; Cory Hathaway at the Los Angeles Athletic Club; and Glen Kila, director, Marae Haʻa Koa Hawaiian Cultural Center, Waiʻanae.

Thanks also to literary agent Rita Rosencrantz, who early on gave me a list of what a good story demanded. Don Wallace, a seasoned writer-editor, pointed me in the right direction. Debra Gwartney reviewed the very first manuscript, and Ben Marcus came in on a second round to push the story forward.

Barbara Pope offered expert guidance about how to take the manuscript to a new level. San Francisco editor Larry Habegger took a look once all the pieces were there; he worked his magic, helping me restructure the narrative. Gordy Grundy was a tremendous help with his overall expertise, photo selection and making old photos look beautiful. Thanks to cartographer Erik Steiner for his map making and hanging in to get it all correct. Mark Bernstein lent legal advice.

I am forever grateful to my patient, amazing editor and collaborator, Constance Hale, scribe par excellence, whose brilliance at turning a phrase, as well as knowledge of and feeling for the Hawaiian culture, brought the *Wave Woman* story alive. She also helped me to develop the psychological layers of a mother who often seemed entirely inscrutable to her daughter.

This is a family story, and my family is both on the page and behind it. Cousins Suzanne Monsoon, Jamie Ingle, Tony Arnold, and Gene Miller generously shared memories. My sister, Gloria, took care of my mother at the end of her life, typed up Betty's haiku, and provided many details of our family story. I also have deep appreciation for my daughters, Marcie and Rennie, who spent three years living with their tutu and gave me valuable insights over many conversations.

The most loving thanks, of course, go to my husband, Bob Liljestrand. He brought my mother into his home for some of her precious last moments, and he gives me never-ending encouragement, insight, and support.

ABOUT THE AUTHOR

Vicky Heldreich Durand first fell in love with Hawaii at age twelve, when she spent a summer with relatives on the island of Molokai. Returning home, she talked her mother Betty into a Hawaiian trip the following summer. By the following winter, the adventurous Betty had moved her two young daughters to Honolulu.

Vicky spent her teenage years surfing with her mother. They competed in the annual Makaha International Surfing Championships. Together, they were invited to Lima, Peru, to promote women's surfing.

Looking back at Vicky and Betty's evolving relationship, Betty always told Vicky that every day was an adventure. Never afraid of the difficult challenges ahead, Betty inspired Vicky to take new challenges and share her mother's story. *Wave Woman* is her first book.

Author photo © Tracy Wright Corvo

PERMISSIONS

Honolulu Star-Bulletin photos from newspaper article

Graham Peake–Don James photo archive

John Clark–Clarence Maki photo archive

Robin Calhoun–Calhoun family photo archive

SHACC Surf Heritage and Cultural Center

Tom Keck photo archive

Drawing of Makaha surf breaks Courtesy of the Preston Peterson Archives

Maps by Erik Steiner

INDEX

SELECTED TITLES FROM SPARKPRESS

SparkPress is an independent boutique publisher delivering high-quality, entertaining, and engaging content that enhances readers' lives, with a special focus on female-driven work. www.gosparkpress.com

The Natives are Restless: A San Francisco dance master takes hula into the twenty-first century, Constance Hale. $40, 978-1-943006-06-9. Journalist Constance Hale presents the largely untold story of the dance tradition of hula, using the twin keyholes of Kumu Patrick Makuakane (a Hawaii-born, San Francisco-based hula master), and his 350-person arts organization. In the background, she weaves the poignant story of an ancient people and the resilience of their culture.

Roots and Wings: Ten Lessons of Motherhood that Helped Me Create and Run a Company, Margery Kraus with Phyllis Piano. $16.95, 978-1-68463-024-0. Margery Kraus, a trailblazing corporate and public affairs professional who became a mother at twenty-one, shares ten lessons from motherhood and leadership that enabled her to create, run, and grow a global company. Her inspiring story of crashing through barriers as she took on increasingly challenging opportunities will have women of all ages cheering.

The Restless Hungarian: Modernism, Madness, and The American Dream, Tom Weidlinger. $16.95, 978-1-943006-96-0. A revolutionary, a genius, and a haunted man . . . The story of the architect-engineer Paul Weidlinger, whose colleagues called him "The Wizard," spans the rise of modern architecture, the Holocaust, and the Cold War. The revelation of hidden Jewish identity propels the author to trace his father's life and adventures across three continents.

Engineering a Life: A Memoir, Krishan K. Bedi. $16.95, 978-1-943006-43-4. A memoir of Krishan Bedi's experiences as a young Indian man in the South in the 1960s, this is a story of one man's perseverance and determination to create the life he'd always dreamed for himself and his family, despite his options seeming anything but limitless.